THE EROS SUTRAS

Volume 3

ORGASMIC MEDITATION

NICOLE DAEDONE

soulmaker | PRESS

Soulmaker Press
soulmakerpress.com

Copyright ©2024 Soulmaker Press

"Orgasmic Meditation" is a trademark of OM IP Co.
used under license by Soulmaker Press.

All rights reserved. No part of this book may be reproduced
in any form without written permission from the publisher.

ISBN: 978-1-961064-16-4 (Luxury edition)
ISBN: 978-1-961064-20-1 (Print on Demand)
ISBN: 978-1-961064-19-5 (eBook)

Library of Congress Cataloging-in-Publication Data
Available Upon Request

Printed in China

10 9 8 7 6 5 4 3 2 1

My capacity to articulate many of the ideas in this book was profoundly impacted by Jim Herriot and Reese Jones who were each willing to dialogue endlessly until the marriage of art and science revealed itself in Eros.

CONTENTS

Preface xi

INTRODUCTION TO PRACTICE

1. Our Relationship to Practice 3
2. The Order of Desire 8
3. The Deeper Desire 11

    Definition of Eros 15
    Definition of Tumescence 17

FOUNDATIONAL APPROACHES

THE FOUR LAWS OF EROS 25

4. Breaking Our Rules 25
5. Playing with Power 28
6. Ambivalence 36
7. Anticipation 38

THE FIVE CORNERSTONES OF ATTENTION 41

8. The Cornerstones 41

THE FIVE CONDITIONS 44

9. Introduction to the Five Conditions 44
10. Evolving Safety 46
11. Evolving Power 49
12. Evolving Connection 52
13. Evolving Variety 54
14. Evolving Extension 57

STROKING

THE SPOT 63

15. The Cartography of the Clitoris 63
16. Just This Stroke 74
17. Finding the Spot 76

HOW TO STROKE 80

18. Life Is an OM 80
19. Intimacy Speaks to Us in Sensation 82
20. Fast Strokes 84
21. Medium-Speed Strokes 87
22. Slow Strokes 88
23. Misusing Speed and What Becomes Available
    through Speed Used Well 91
24. Pressure: Anchoring the Mind in Feeling 94
25. Heavy Pressure 99
26. Medium Pressure 101
27. Light Pressure 103
28. Giving Good Heavy Pressure Is an Art 105

29.	Downstrokes	108
30.	Understanding Downstrokes through OM	110
31.	Upstrokes	112
32.	The Felt Experience of Pressures, Speeds, and Directions	115
33.	Understanding Length	118
34.	The Strokes	119

Following the Sensation 123

35.	Turning on the Spot	123
36.	Unconditionality	126
37.	Peak to Go Down, Get More Power, and Go Higher	128
38.	Go in the Direction the Sensation Is Going	130

Working with Hindrances 132

39.	Introduction to the Three Distractions	132
40.	Sweetness	134
41.	Protest	136
42.	Brokenness	138
43.	Taking Comfort in Suffering or Healing	140
44.	How Two Sensitivities Engage	150
45.	Beneath the Fog Is Everything	158
46.	Meeting Our Erotic Self Beneath the Fog	160

OM Mastery 163

| 47. | The Advancements of Attention | 163 |
| 48. | The Three Levels of OM | 167 |

THE EIGHT STAGES

49. Learning the Eight Stages Is Learning to Follow the Body 169
50. Introduction to the Eight Stages 171
51. The First Stage: Climax 173
52. The Second Stage: Resolution 182
53. The Third Stage: Restoration 187
54. The Fourth Stage: Turn-On 191
55. The Fifth Stage: The Peak 197
56. The Sixth Stage: Expression 202
57. The Seventh Stage: Play 207
58. The Eighth Stage: Stillness 213

The Container and Form of Orgasmic Meditation 217
On Language and Terms 241
Key Definitions 243
The Eros Sutras Volumes 253

PREFACE

In 1997, I met a guy with tattoo sleeves and a motorcycle. Whatever eyebrows may be raised I should assure you he had also read *Zen Mind, Beginner's Mind*—or at least I'd seen a copy of it in his backpack. He invited me to an event—I didn't know what it was. Dismounting his bike outside the venue, he put his hand on the small of my back and invited me to a demonstration of a woman in orgasm. I had no idea what that meant.

It was in the Richmond District of San Francisco in a beautiful house with taupe walls and dark brown curtains. Candlelight refracted through hurricane glass holders cast the room in a warm cream color. There was a Gustav Klimt painting above the fireplace, and in front of me, there was a massage table covered by a perfectly ironed white sheet. Two women stood on either side, like ballerinas in their Diane von Furstenberg wrap dresses. They were poised but entirely wild.

At the time, I was a graduate teaching associate in women's studies at San Francisco State University and a serious feminist. A postmodern-feminist-deconstructionist-lesbian, with my "U.S. out of my uterus!" T-shirt and my Take Back the Night placard, carried while I marched without any shirt on at all. That's the person who walked into that room; it's not the woman who walked out.

A man entered, followed by one of the most breathtaking women I had ever seen and not solely for her physical beauty. Dressed in a gold robe, she had Catherine Deneuve cheeks and blond hair brushed back exposing translucent skin. Something else emanated from her. I couldn't look away. I couldn't think. They faced each other beside the table doing something called a heat exercise, but I couldn't focus or make sense of anything they said.

The woman removed her robe and mounted the massage table. The man turned and addressed the audience. "Just notice," he said. "That's all you have to do tonight is just notice. Notice she may have a flush in her cheeks. She may have swelling. She may have a pool of ejaculate. You may notice some shivering, the activation of the involuntary musculature. Just do your best to notice. Notice what she looks like now, because she may look different at the end."

The naked woman lay back on the table, her head on a pillow, legs butterflied open and supported by a cushion under each thigh. He stood to her right and bent over slightly. He put his right thumb in her introitus and with his left forefinger he began to stroke the upper left hand quadrant of her clitoris. While he was stroking her, I made my very best effort to notice. I just kept noticing. I was noticing. I was noticing. I was noticing and then all of a sudden . . . I was hit with a blast unlike anything I had ever known.

I'm not really much of a hiker, but once, on walking up the very low mountain of Calaveras, there had been a snow and I remember that feeling of clarity from taking in the pristine air, free from self-concern, immersed in eternal space. I felt connected to everything. The mind stilled. That kind of clarity. Not a single thought. Nothing.

And then *boom*, I was back. Judging. Comparing. Fixing. *I'm more powerful than these women. I'm a real feminist. Cover her up. She doesn't need to be exploited by the male gaze.* The thoughts were choking me and then *boom*, I got hit again.

I was riveted. I couldn't avert my eyes, I couldn't move my head. I could sense that all of us seemed to be in the same state. We were moving in unison, connected, possessed, by this woman who was doing nothing other than being completely vulnerable. Then it struck me, *wait a minute. Maybe THAT is feminine power*. Not fighting the patriarchy, but the willful engagement in exquisitely tuned receptivity.

There's a term, *duende*, a quality of being passionately irresistible, in flamenco dance. The young flamenco dancers are very demonstrative, very dramatic. But as they become more seasoned, their powerful heat rivets the watcher. They become increasingly still, pulling everyone to the edge of their seats, holding them in suspense. For a dancer like this, one bat of an eyelash moves an entire room.

Receptive, attentive stillness: I saw in this moment a kind of power that wasn't usually acknowledged as such. But I knew in that moment it was the kind of power I wanted, the gravitational force that comes from vulnerability, that would move the world around me, rather than punching my way up or down. But, being a smart woman, I also knew it was dangerous. It was dangerous to carry that kind of power because that is real power. And the moment I realized that, I was knocked out while still on my feet. Everything went blank.

I came to in a fit of self-consciousness. I'm nearly six feet tall; the women around me were sexy, elegant, svelte, and petite. I felt like a gumball machine bobble in platforms and a leopard print jumpsuit with my Jennifer Aniston hair. I agonized over the rolls on my belly. I felt like a drag queen and they looked like *Breakfast at Tiffany's*. The comparison was torture. I searched the room for my date, for his affirmation, and I was again hit for the last time.

I had been treating sexuality like it was a second-class citizen to be used for the extraction of things, position, power. In that moment, I saw what this energy actually is. It clarifies and heals. It's not a big show, and it's not about transacting in any way. It is not about what it can get you, like a better grade, a role in a play, a break from a traffic cop, a boyfriend or a husband or girlfriend or a baby or a dishwasher.

Chögyam Trungpa wrote a book called *Cutting Through Spiritual Materialism*. It begins with the notion that real spiritual practice is when the limitations of the grasping, self-centered, self-conscious ego are dissolved, unleashing freedom, deep connectedness, and joy. But the self-grasping, me-first ego doesn't die easily. It can co-opt just about anything, including the spirituality that's there to dissolve it. When our spirituality doesn't cut deep enough, the ego dresses itself up in outward signs of purity: a mindful demeanor; prayer beads around the wrist or draped from the neck; hemp clothes and vegan shoes. Those who do this make sure you know they are *spiritual*. We think this is what spiritual looks like.

In the same way, we think we know what sexual looks like: a leopard-print unitard, teddies, vibrators, jade eggs, feathers, whips. But I started to wonder if this wasn't sexual materialism, a parallel to spiritual materialism. And just as spiritual materialism isn't the real spirituality of unleashing the heart and mind, sexual materialism isn't about the power, freedom, and authenticity of sexuality I was seeing play out before me.

I was lost in rumination when the woman being stroked sat up. It was over. And the man was right: she did look different. She was more light than woman. I remember thinking, *I don't know how she does that, but that's what I want to do. That's who I want to be.*

The feminist in me who believed she was powerless in the face of oppression died that night. My own volition was finally awake.

◆ ◆ ◆

John Perry Barlow says the difference between love and true love is the difference between a very large number and infinity. For me, the difference between sex and Orgasmic Meditation (OM) is the difference between a very large number and infinity. OM opens into a kind of infinity. It liberates you of the mind that's keeping track, the mind that compares, the mind that believes we are powerless and trapped in suffering.

I have spent most of my adult life studying, practicing, and developing OM as an attention-training practice that brings human beings into alignment with the fundamental pure energy of sexuality.

In OM, there are ten spots, two directions, three pressures, three speeds. The aim is to meet, in pitch-perfect response, whatever the stroke is.

Each spot has a particular frequency associated with it. One can see the clitoris as a clock with the twelve o'clock spot at the top, the six o'clock spot at the base. The one o'clock spot is considered *the* spot. You return there to orient, find neutrality with what is called the bread-and-butter stroke. The twelve o'clock spot, especially with light pressure and light speed, confers a sense of reverence. The six o'clock spot, a sense of deep earthiness. The nine o'clock spot, dark and mystical. And so on in various gradations, depending on pressure and speed.

Attention is trained through resonance to open to, meet, and receive the stroke. When this is done well, it doesn't matter the stroke—stroker and strokee become one, a gateway in consciousness opens, and entry into that place occurs. All becomes bliss irrespective of what it is. Reverence is as blissful as dark and gritty, the basic everyday sensation of the three o'clock spot becomes sublime.

We all have tendencies or preferences that make our particular signature. The aim is to fully develop that signature as a carrier signal while developing all other spots, speeds, and pressures in such a way that you have full optionality, while having a unique gift to offer. My frequency, for example, is the two o'clock spot. The stroke on that spot evokes what we might think of as the various expressions of love: ranging from a feeling of deep sex to compassion. Heavier pressure and it's sex; lighter and it's compassion.

We all have a weak spot and may spend years opening it so that attention is liberated to the same degree as what one is naturally proficient in. When this occurs, it is not linear. There is a phase transition and the lights go on in a way they never go off again. All flavors are now bliss while maintaining their particularity.

Encoded in each stroke are the instructions of how to respond. You can't figure it out any way other than to get the stroke, listen, and attune. You learn to move the attention toward or away from, make the aperture more open or closed, push out or draw in. At the point that one is "lit up," the response is second nature; it occurs in ambient attention rather than directly. It's always fun but a new level of fun starts there. You never know where you'll end up but you know you have the capacity to find bliss there even in the strokes most often avoided—heavy and grinding or frenetic or a certain hovering or absence from the stroker. Preference and aversion dissolve as one learns to meet the stroke. In other words, attention affixes to the potential rather than fixing, and the result is that neuroses dissolve in the wake.

Again, this takes years, decades, or lifetimes. There is no final mastering it, just as one does not master an instrument. You can always refine. You discover tiny "stuck spots" that invite release. Mastery in this case is deliberately going into what is stuck without pushing, with the delight of knowing that what seems difficult is only stuckness and if one remains with it, it will always open into greater bliss—more complex and vivified. What was stuck, when brought into circulation, becomes fuel.

The demo is one's declaration that they have met the requirements to find bliss anywhere; and yet it is just the beginning. A shift occurs. A woman learns to strengthen her signal to "stroke from reception," to call in. She also learns to actively seek out what is difficult or unfamiliar. The positive reinforcement upon opening to where one was closed is so great that the art at this point lies in throwing oneself into the unfamiliar and attuning the gyroscope. Now you know in practice, not in theory, that you can find joy.

The practice is pure play. Challenges occur in getting attached to a particular stroke or field, especially at the peak point that naturally occurs, as life is impermanent. You peak at the moment the next stroke will be less sensational. If one grips, sensation not only decreases with the light that confers bliss diminishing but it becomes painful until one opens to the new spot. The second you open again, bliss is restored, and the "new" is fresh and exhilarating.

I often say I've lived my life on the tip of a finger, from an actual physical finger to an ever-increasingly-subtle invisible finger.

There is always a spot that is the most resonant. When perfectly attuned, the stroker and strokee hear it, attune to it, and the pure intimacy, the experience of mutual emptiness occurs: connected to the totality, no sense of self, eternal.

Upon reemergence, the intimacy is unreal. A knowing and trust, a sense of minds merged to move in lockstep together. More practice is more seamless merging until the two sense this in all things, and together, radiate it into the world. This radiation lights up the world around it. Others are lit up around the field of the two, but even when separate there is no separation.

Stroking has its own set of instructions. But ultimately, there is a transceiving where, like an instrument, it's unclear where the stroke is issuing from: her invisible frequency or the stroker's finger.

This abstracts into one's experience of the world. The fast hard stroke of Harlem becomes the same bliss as the great meditators' caves in

Tibet. Jealousy as electric as a kiss. Having as pleasurable as wanting. All is welcomed without cutting anything off. Rage is primordial sex when fully received. Rather than deny or redirect or transmute, one feels all the way through. Eventually, every last bit of it reveals itself as undifferentiated love, but only if you meet it on its terms, which might look like anything but. You don't need to eliminate the sense of self but instead become the self that is the totality. This way one can issue effective care and compassion on the terms of what one is meeting without imposing or dismissing. You do not expect another to come to your place on high; you meet them in intimacy. Again, this opens the gate to where you would bring them. This allows people to be free, as who they are, and to feel spacious love.

This is my art and I pride myself on my capacity to open to, add, direct with reception whatever comes my way. Sometimes it takes my gyroscope a second to adjust to a new stroke and see how I could open to or love even this, what needs to be let go of and what needs a greater pull.

I do this by going into my one o'clock spot of solitude until what is called for emerges. When vibrant clarity comes, the procedure is complete and I'm ready again for any stroke.

These Sutras are a result of so much of what I've learned. I have spent decades codifying and clarifying them in the hopes that you may discover the true power, freedom, and love that exists within pure Erotic energy.

INTRODUCTION TO PRACTICE

1.
OUR RELATIONSHIP TO PRACTICE

To endeavor in practice is to engage in the art of "making sacred"—carving out space in time where the unconscious may be made conscious.

Humans have long sought contact with the Mystery that undergirds the whole of life. In the material world, we might build a cathedral or temple as a space set apart, hallowed. Or we might construct symphony halls and studios to house the inflow of the creative force—the intention being to provide a container such that the profane can undergo the conversion into the profound.

To endeavor in practice is to shift from a state of being as an isolated, closed system, recycling habituated patterns of thought and action into one based on a relationship between self and the Mystery.

Put simply, practice is the vehicle through which we convert tumescence into Eros. Within the walls of practice, the vital energies of the unknown can make contact with the default survival patterns that are passively grooved into us. Beneath these patterns lie the untapped potential of our humanity.

To shift oneself into living as a dynamic relationship rather than a static reality is no small matter. To do so is to work as a sculptor, carving away what is *not* us, so that who we truly are is revealed and ultimately liberated from the confines of static identity.

We fundamentally exchange systems of order. On their own, the pre-practice, default rational and ideological systems we employ that precede this shift, leave little room for the Mystery to circulate. Instead, they dictate that we receive the world in the boxes, categories, and classifications that we seem to have been born with. Information and perceptions are sorted accordingly in terms of the preexisting. Reality is made to fit into our constructs. We take reality in.

In a practice-based approach to life, the aim first and foremost is to dissolve the preexisting so that we may then offer ourselves to know reality on reality's terms. This means our practice exists first to be destructive. We take down the walls, the filters, the sorting mechanisms, and the stagnant energy that blunts our contact with the living, breathing, self-evident truth of each moment.

We make ourselves available for reality to communicate itself to us, rather than demand it deliver itself in forms we're familiar with and then protest when it will not.

And so, at its foundation, all practice rests upon humility. Not the head-bowed feigning of humility that typifies spiritual tradition, but the humility of admitting the futility and cost of our selfish demands.

Having been driven by them so long, we come to the hard-won realization that no matter how valiant the effort of the will rooted in the self may be, self-will employed in opposition to reality will eventually lose every time. Our soul yearns for us to learn this lesson experientially; and indeed, we repeat it as many times as we require in order to accept that it is not so much virtuous as it is practical to remain with this humility. We find that it renders us willing to relate with life as an interconnected participant, not a would-be director.

Over time this humility matures and presents not only as the willingness to receive and be altered by deeper truth, but by an unwavering fidelity to it. It evolves further into a willingness to release anything that does not align with the flow of truth, and finally employs us in the activities that are our nature: ease, joy, and incandescence.

Humility, not often associated with thrill, becomes one when we discover how to move in pitch-perfect response to constantly shifting and ever-emerging truth. Being at once rooted in the truth and moving with it confers a sense of dynamic stillness . . . and from this stillness we dissolve into the clear radiance that is the substance of the Mystery itself. This is making love, where the self melts in the warmth of the light we have sought. This is the promise of humility.

◆ ◆ ◆

Before all else, our primary relationship then is with truth, and at the root of all truth is love. Truth is the vehicle that will deliver us to love every time. The tumescent, pre-practice mind is not engaged in a relationship *with*, so much as it is interested in a dominion *over*. When we live under its rule, our default programs always attempt to drive us to a peaceful slumber—physical comfort and pleasure free from irritation. We are offered a surface-level life with a promise of safety so long as we follow the rules; the first rule being to remain on the surface and suppress the itch to discover what lies beneath.

In practice, we carve out access points to the deeper dimensions of truth, gradually flooding the surface with love from below. At the beginning, each new channel we forge provides a temporary reprieve from the dry, arid surface—a place we can enter when we need some refreshment. The effect is cumulative. We discover love wants to be liberated in every facet of our lives. The surface, now weakened and no longer able to delude us, washes out completely, and the surface-dwelling "you" is absorbed into and becomes this truth.

We are relieved of our self—that pain-manufacturing machinery comprised of the ideas, beliefs, attitudes, and preferences that keep us buoying on the surface. We can finally sink down and know the true dimensions of our self in the depths—in our uniqueness and in our universality.

In the pre-practice mind, we must defend our rightness. Tumescent thinking is based on the rational, so arguments will be made against us, which we must in turn overpower. Everything is assailable. In the practice mind, defense only works to keep us from our birthright of freedom. Our practice then becomes the free person's means of cultivating their plot of land. The composting of old ideas eventually bears the fruits of realization. Our relationship to this land, to our practice, is itself a practice.

◆ ◆ ◆

Remember, the root of all truth is love, and the root of all practice is love as well. We practice for the love of practice, the discovery, the uncovering. We can either trek terrain like a mule, trudging along hoping for a carrot, or like an adventurer who loves the path unconditionally.

We are not practicing to become a good or even better person, to find peace or feel better. We are not practicing to acquire new skills or assume the identity of "practitioner." We are not even practicing to feel more, or increase our sensitivity or connection, or any of the various outcomes that often occur as the result of practice. We practice in order to liberate the active, sentient, intelligent, and life-seeking aspect of Eros known as desire.

Deep within each of us lies a yearning. True desire, when activated and followed, becomes an agent of what we most yearn for: a living, breathing relationship with the Mystery.

That yearning is the Mystery seeking itself. When, through care in practice, we offer ourselves (our attention, time, frustrations, vulnerability, inexperience; essentially our heart), we are met with access to the heart of Eros.

Where outside of it we were confused, irritated, and out of focus, we are now granted entry into the interior world wherein lies a living presence—the source that naturally orders, clarifies, vivifies, and feeds that hunger of the heart: the need to know, to touch, to be made whole by this force that surrounds us and is now moving through us. We come home, curing the homesickness of which all suffering is a symptom, and inhabit our life on its terms.

The tumescent fixing that consumes everyday life resolves on its own. We discover that it, along with judging and comparing, dissolves upon contact with our practice mind. They are rendered unnecessary as that chronic background sense of "something's wrong" is now made right. All along, it was seeking for this contact with itself.

Practice then is where we allow this deep-seated hunger to draw us to sustenance. We are drawn by this desire to this living presence, this source, to be changed, informed, emboldened, and attuned in the process in order to access more through this exchange with life itself. The Mystery draws us ever more out of known patterns, habits, and needs into the only thing that will truly gratify: the spacious field where we get to see our experience through life's eyes. Here the dramas, the jealousy, the love, the passion, the angst, the isolation, the grief, and the yearning play out as rich and beautiful textures and sensations, not as problems and obstacles to be solved, but as rhythms and notes to be first felt and then played through the instrument of the body.

And so develops a respect, a care, a tending to the body as the instrument through which all experience is known. Each day a tuning, an inquiry into what would facilitate this pitch-perfect response to life, brings about this sense of presence. Not in spite of the body, but because of and through this body, through its tenderness and frailties, we know the whole of life from the most subtle to the most extreme. And so we make it our life's work to incarnate.

This is where we start, with gentle care, attending to and including the body where we might otherwise like to go faster or higher if we were without its discomforts or drives. Instead, we make the body our particular point of access. Rather than going "up and out," we move into and through the body and, as a result, are rewarded by Eros's first experiential lesson: truth is whole and can only be accessed when everything, even the lesser, the slower, the lower, is loved and included.

We are rewarded by the sense of devotion and fidelity that only the "lower" (the body) can confer. Our body becomes the most loyal friend and guide. We develop a trust in life we may have never known as we enter a wholly honest relationship. People spend their lives lying to their bodies, telling them they need to be other than they are or that they are somehow unnecessary or inconvenient. Our bodies forgive us and reveal a whole new possibility as the truth is revealed: our bodies never lie.

2.
THE ORDER OF DESIRE

A body well attended to desires order and will happily give itself over to protocols that can effectively substitute for the vigilance aspect of consciousness: the sentinel of the mind that cannot let go until the basics of survival are looked after; until we know we are safe. We cannot let go or give ourselves over to the Mystery until the part of our mind that is constantly and chronically scanning for danger knows it can relax.

We have two primary methods for relaxing vigilance. The first is to feel internally safe enough regardless of our circumstances. Otherwise, we can create certain conditions that serve as an extension of this aspect of the mind. We can agree to follow a set of protocols, as protocols establish an external sense of containment. Through time, location, and repetition, we carve out a sense of space that, because it is reliable and predictable, allows the mind to relax and let go. Our sense of trust now extends beyond the confines of our body and into this deliberate space. We feel held by it because we have carved it out by repeatedly returning to a specific location within a specific timeframe and following a set pattern.

To return and adhere to the protocols we established again and again has nothing to do with duty but instead with developing a trust, a familiarity. We carve something out of the invisible that becomes palpable—a sanctuary where we can take off the armor, the protection, the self-consciousness that is constantly checking that we are okay, and instead devote that attention to discovery. Each time we adhere to the protocols and agreements we set, we fortify the sanctuary that much more, so we can let go that much more deeply. This is a safety built through trust, trust that we will return, that we will respect, that we will listen.

Our practice and the Mystery we contact within kindles our sense of fidelity. We come when we are called, tend to our experience with great care while we are inside of it, and leave when our time is up. The art of practice, though, aims to establish a sound economy within the mind. The figuring, vacillating, wondering, and debating that our pre-practice mind occupies itself with are premium expenditures; they take up a great deal of energy that could otherwise be dedicated to our practice. Over time we learn to draw the energy down from the mind and into the body where we invest in venturing and exploring, sensing, and coming to know what we encounter. A practice is a loosely worn decision we make to return again and again. We build our sanctuary of trust with the Mystery that we may be granted proportional access to it. What we meet in its depths leaves its indelible mark upon us: we walk in the world as a beacon of ease, joy, and radiance. We so enjoy where our attention could go if it were not employed in debate that we preset parameters to take out all that guesswork.

First, we carve out a space that is wholly dedicated to the endeavor of OM. Our relationship with this space will be what sustains us as we build our world of practice. It will be the literal ground of our experience. We will relate to it as a good friend. We will place our physical bodies in this physical space and practice the art of developing trust with our environment through the attentive care we offer. We notice and tend to minute details in the space. This space becomes hallowed through our attention and, as a result, it comes alive. It becomes something we do not merely enter but something we interact with. We are attentive to the elements that come together to create an atmosphere, and we allow our senses to guide us. The lighting, the scent, the sounds, the feel of it all come together in a symphonic way. When carefully attended to, these sensory elements do what a practice space is meant to do: create an environment for the body to sink into simple, natural, congruent beauty.

We include nothing opulent that overwhelms the senses, but also take care not to overlook anything that keeps the senses vigilant. Soon the care we put into our practice environment grows so palpable, it radiates the field our practice exists within. Eros needs her fair share of this simple, organic beauty to emerge into.

Next, we carve out the scaffolding of our sanctuary through time. The outer walls define when we practice, and the inner walls determine for how long. The body, deeply obedient by nature, will follow whatever path we offer it. Setting a daily time for practice clears the way for us to move into and out of contact with the Mystery with greater ease. The fretting part of the mind can relax when it knows what to do and when. Time serves as something for the mind to organize around where it might otherwise fall into a state of entropy, an organizing factor that calls in all our resources at once.

Determining the amount of time we will practice relaxes the everyday mind. The mind can trust we will return from our foray with the Mystery to take care of our on-the-ground needs: rest, nutrition, hydration, the very things that make our foray possible. We are building a trust, a bridge between two complementary aspects: our relationship with the Mystery and our basic human self. We shift the relationship between those two wherever they may be at odds; the protocols make it safe to move between both. They can each reap the mutual benefit of the other having what it needs to feel safe. Our internal tension rapidly deescalates when we acknowledge that the aspect that yearns for contact with the Mystery needs uninterrupted space and time, while the everyday self needs to know it will not be forgotten and will be respected. This is what setting time and following it can offer.

Again, these are not hard-and-fast rules. Instead, they are ways to develop a relationship and trust so the whole of our being has what it needs to live in a state of fulfillment: freedom and security.

3.
THE DEEPER DESIRE

As we approach practice, it is key to continually return to the deeper desire: to remember, and through remembering touch the moment when we knew we had been called. Eros, creativity, and the Mystery do not respond well to demands. Duty, obligation, and the forcing of oneself that often denotes a rigorous practice are approaches that simply do not work in this realm. We will find ourselves in a space devoid of meaning going through the motions, locked out of the Mystery, and at best, chalking up time.

We are practicing in order to touch, interact with, and be filled by Eros, remembering that what activates Eros and opens her door is *desire*. Integrity, respect, and following rules matter little to Eros. Not because Eros lacks a system of order or is messy or chaotic. Quite the contrary. Integrity, respect, and rule-following are simply what we default to when we are not guided by something deeper. Those are imperatives that must be maintained by the will, the notion being that without them we would become slothful or cause harm. The problem with this reasoning is that when our limited rational faculty is driving, we will always be "performing" things we do not want to do, even when they are beneficial.

Desire, on the other hand—a power we all share just as we all share human suffering—asks us to live from a deeper drive. Desire wants more for us than a life where we merely follow orders and comply with a particular idea of how to conduct ourselves. Instead, we are invited into a level of Erotic adulthood where we must learn experientially by trying things out and facing consequences. Should we accept, we come to know the deeper truths for ourselves. We live them out and are fortified with the experiential "why" of higher-order truths, rather than being forced to rely on what an external authority would tell us so that we are absolved of the responsibility of our own knowing.

More importantly, we must prove ourselves willing to hold the weight of our desire. We want intimacy with life, and this is the key. We may act as though it is not our desire to enter into this relationship and that we are merely in servitude, going through the motions in order to satisfy some demand or burden that has been placed upon us in a dramatic display of martyrdom. The practice of Eros is extraordinarily challenging, demanding, and complex, but in admitting our desire to take on this endeavor, we forego our parent/child relationship with practice. We are admitting we do it for ourselves simply because we want to. The difficulty is precisely what makes it great. The fact that it is so black-and-white in how it works is what moves us to our edge. If we give everything, Eros arrives. If we do not give everything, we can get everything except the one thing we are there for.

Eros is entirely impersonal amid all of our mental back doors, reservations, holdouts, stratagems, and anything-but-thats. We are welcome to hold on to whatever we are protecting. There is no external dogma or discipline to say we cannot have the things we would hold out for. However, Eros is very clear: "Those, or Eros." If we put Eros first, those things may or may not come. If we put those things first, Eros will not come. And while we may even have those things, we will not find the gratification in them that only Eros can bestow. Eros drives a hard bargain, but in the long run, it is a relief to have such incredibly clear instructions and feedback.

Eros is not a middle path but a path of dynamic tension born between extremes. Eros is in no way about moderation bell-curve spirituality. Extremes are not excluded here. Eros holds that no "truth" is self-evident. Instead, all truth is earned through experience: the interaction, the working with, the coming to know life on its terms.

"Integrity"-based truths are empty; they are ideas devoid of the content of experience. They are a way to avoid trouble, not a way to know life. We can maintain a safe distance from an objective relationship with life when we merely offer it respectful distance or dutiful response. Eros says this is not enough and will leave us to our safety and intellectual understanding. We will be left with a formula (not creativity), propriety (not relationship), and discipline (not practice). We will not have practice because what we are practicing is devoid of this intimacy with life, with its extremes and intensities. It is an experience of humility to recognize we must show up on life's terms, not try to have it show up on ours. These performances of integrity, discipline, and respect disguise the fact we are not giving Eros the one thing it wants: us. And until we do, we can spend our lives in what we may call practice and never touch the instrument. We may be able to intellectually describe and even instruct others on practice and never actually touch it. We might fool many, but *we* will always know.

So we return to the only force that can melt us down enough to be moved in practice: desire. We allow ourselves to feel, to admit how we yearn to touch, to know, to be changed by contact with Eros, with life. Rather than dragging ourselves to practice with a self-congratulatory martyrdom, we let desire draw us through our resistance into the only place we want to be. We do not perform being good and kind and generous. We do not "set boundaries" and defend. We instead allow this force to draw forth our goodness, to so finely tune our senses in order to detect the perfect resonance and find the boundary that naturally exists. We have no need for discipline when we admit we want to feel good, and that this desire is the vehicle that will drive us there. Discipline is extra, but desire will forge us into joyous rigor.

What we discover is that desire wants more than any human standard could ever ask of us in terms of morality. Morality is far too low a bar. Desire wants a generosity of love and attention from us, an openness and availability, a sensitivity and response, a natural expression of genuine care. It trains us to grow toward these behaviors, positively reinforcing us through greater access to Eros when we exhibit them. There is no cheating desire. Any attempt to pass off performative behaviors as the real thing interrupts the feedback loop.

Desire desires good, hard work, hyper-focus, and the most exquisite care of not just other human beings, not just of all living forms, but of *all* things. It desires not the checklist of integrity but the clarity of congruency. It wants us to work life with our own hands. A practice left in the hands of desire will work us out harder than any finite discipline ever could. And we will not be left with the consolation prize of self-respect but with the gratitude that we have been liberated from the limitations of mere self.

To truly begin practice, one admission is required: that we want this. We want it bad. We want to dive in and give ourselves over. Until we do, we are just biding time. We may as well do it now. Or if we can, we should do everything in our power to leave the path of Eros. Anything in between is just being caught in the breakers.

DEFINITION OF EROS

Eros is an impersonal, primal force of nature that arises from the ground of being and draws us into contact with life, changing us and life as a result. It is the unfolding process of this drawing together, touching, and mutual altering, and it is the network of interiorly connected essences that arises in response to this contact.

Eros is the filament that runs through all of life, aiming for a harmony that will unite the primordial forces of the soul with the spiritual ideals of the above in a delicate balance.

We know Eros through a dimension of perception that opens and shifts the ordinary to the extraordinary. Occurring as a charged, magnetized emptiness, it draws forth and is moved by what will bring us into and through our most cherished notions in order to restore wholeness and cultivate this perceptive capacity.

It rests on the nexus of paradox, in that wholeness is found by organizing around a radiant absence. And we know it not directly, but implicitly, the way we know electricity through a bulb as light, or through a radiator as heat, or through a vehicle as motion.

Operating by a set of laws equal and complementary to the more conventional and familiar laws of the rational system of order, Eros connects us to and through its various realms by way of a chaotic order and a nonrational intelligence. It draws us in through the power of desire, impulse, hunger, yearning, intuition, and passion, and orients us to the primordial chaos that is the source of its power.

DEFINITION OF TUMESCENCE

Tumescence, derived from the Latin word *tumere*, meaning to swell, arises when we consciously or unconsciously redirect Erotic energy away from its natural course. This struggle between our innate desire for unity and pleasure and our self-crafted notions of right and wrong leads to the accumulation of unused Erotic energy within us. Unmet internal feelings, including fear, desire, joy, repulsion, and love, remain unabsorbed, accumulating within our bodies and minds, akin to plaque in an artery. Left unprocessed, this buildup disrupts the Erotic body, the wellspring of creativity and vitality.

In the ordinary course of things, the Erotic body possesses an innate processing system, similar to emotional digestion, dynamically converting stagnant Erotic energy into available life force. Energy is neither created nor destroyed—only transformed into something else. When the Erotic body functions correctly, Erotic impulses and desires seamlessly transform into a flowing, continuously renewed, creative life force. We can absorb significant impact in this state while remaining happy.

However, when Eros is suppressed over time, our creative life force becomes tumescent, turning inward and causing a feeling of swelling, inflammation, and irritability. This sense of tumescence resembles a persistent background alarm, leaving the body in a heightened state of arousal while the mind expends precious energy attempting to silence it. If allowed to accumulate, tumescence can lead to destructive consequences, rendering us reactive and explosive. In these early stages, if a friend draws attention to our tumescence, we can still hear them and take corrective action—such as engaging in an OM, meditating, or indulging in a relaxing bath—to release the contraction. Failure to do so propels us into the higher stages of tumescence: diagnosis, prescription, and ultimately, sickness.

In these advanced stages, dynamism wanes, supplanted by rigidity, while our critical faculties expand, and our parasympathetic system shuts down, leaving us in a state of inertia. This deceleration may manifest as mania, a frenzied slowness that estranges us from our dynamic core. Tumescence also forges emotional armor, stifling passion, flow, intimacy, and creativity. In these later stages, if a friend points out our tumescence, we interpret it as an affront and take no action to restore our dynamism.

On the surface, tumescence may appear as an existential condition, a vague, nameless longing for the unknown, suggesting a quest for a deeper self-definition. But this is far from the truth. Once sufficient tumescence accumulates and solidifies, it becomes a self-sustaining entity, siphoning our life force. It feeds off us internally, draining our vitality, and externally, by orchestrating situations and provocations beyond our conscious control. Tumescence assumes various physical or emotional guises, seeking to draw more energy toward itself. This condition is contagious, perpetuating itself by feeding on the tumescence in others. In states of heightened tumescence, we often find ourselves surrounded by individuals steeped in complaints, sicknesses, and diagnoses. However, clarity is also infectious. In the early stages of tumescence, we tend to be amidst people who more readily return to a state of flow, dynamism, and clarity.

The feminine essence, when in its tumescent form, manifests as rigidity, annoyance, unsatisfied cravings, dissatisfaction, agitation, lethargy, guilt, anxiety, and irritability, often accompanied by heightened sensitivity to criticism. Conversely, the masculine essence, in its tumescent state, gives rise to feelings of helplessness, inadequacy, impotence, self-loathing, anger, and rapaciousness, frequently leading to excessive drive in social and career pursuits.

Common "Problems"

The tumescent mind would rather be right than be happy, so it develops an idea that something is lacking. The following is a list of questions meant to help us understand the ways tumescence typically operates:

- When we believe we are hopeless, is this belief created by actively denying situations and experiences that give us hope, focusing instead on our inadequacies?

- When we feel less than capable, are we really demanding a position of dependency, turning away from learning the skills that would have us become capable?

- When we say we are unwanted or don't belong, have we created a barbed-wire fence around ourselves? Are we living in a position of against-ness that repels others? Do we justify being unkind by saying we are being rejected, not the other way around?

- When we feel worthless, have we created this feeling by avoiding activities that build a sense of worth and continuing activities that drain it, using our "worthlessness" as justification?

- When we believe we are only wanted for X (our money, skills, body), have we created this perception by offering X, often in an attempt to maintain control through X, and by negating any evidence we are wanted for something beyond it?

- When we are kicked out, have we created a situation where it's untenable to include us?

- When we feel as though we are not enough, have we created this feeling inside ourselves by only showing up with a minimum amount of effort?

- When we feel we are never good enough, have we created this feeling by not doing our best or not giving our all?

- When we feel invisible or believe we don't have a voice, have we created this feeling because we have remained concealed by hiding or not speaking? Do we get angry when we perceive we are unseen or unheard, using that experience to justify not speaking, thereby creating a vicious cycle? Alternatively, when we do come out and are seen or heard, do we come out with resentment or vindictiveness, which makes it difficult for others to listen to us?

- When we frequently feel "messed up," is this because we continue to create messes by indulging in behavior that messes us up, and do we then fail to clean up the messes we've made?

- When we think we are "too much," is this thought created by not developing boundaries that stop at other people's limits?

- When we think we are unlovable, is this thought created by rejecting love from others?

- When we think we are too good for certain situations, activities, or people, is this a feeling of false superiority, created by spending our time cataloging everyone else's defects and focusing on our own positive attributes?

- When we feel we never get what we want, is this feeling created by focusing on what we don't have while denying what we have?

- When we are always in trouble, is this state of affairs created by provoking it either explicitly or under the radar?

- When we don't feel respected, is this created by empty, exaggerated talk while failing to do the work to secure the truth, facts, self-knowledge, and stability that command respect?

- When we think we are the only one who knows something, is this perception created by discounting what everyone else knows?

- When we think we know better than everyone else, is this thought created by denying our own faults and only looking at other people's failures?

FOUNDATIONAL
APPROACHES

THE FOUR LAWS OF EROS

4.
BREAKING OUR RULES

The object of Orgasmic Meditation (OM) is the realization of the *Erotic self*, the self that arises from the ground of being in its totality, so that it may carry out the specific and unique calling within. This Erotic self exists in direct opposition to the rational aim of operating in accord with a standard, externalized set of ideas we experience as inner prohibitions, or rules.

With Eros, it is vital to know the rules of realization so we can break them in a beneficial way; if we are to realize in our totality, then break them we must. The skill lies in our capacity to break the rules within a deeper understanding of how to do so as an articulation of our unique expression, and in a way that benefits those around us. Mere breaking or following the rules is considered sloth in OM because while mere rule-following creates rigidity, mere rule-breaking creates disconnection. We always aim for flexible connection—connection that abides by Erotic principles.

For many people, the first rule we break is the rule to always follow rules. For others, following the deeper code of Eros involves breaking the rules governing interdependence and connection. Those who have leaned heavily on independence or autonomy will find themselves rendered useless when collaboration is required.

In OM, we are playing with differentiation and integration. Differentiation implies a movement toward what makes each of us distinct and separate. Integration explores this differentiation within the context of connection with others. When we're able to bridge these two poles, we become a more complex human being, with the skill that enables us to access not only the known parts of the self but also the Mystery that lies within.

Around every interior prohibition lies a charged barrier—charged in the sense that we hold a strong positively or negatively charged belief along with the prohibition. In OM, the way we expand our sensation of space, freedom, and aliveness is that we directly aim our attention at these barriers, detonating the charge that surrounds them. The barrier protecting the idea may go up in flames, and the energy released becomes available to us as raw power. As the barrier comes down, it liberates the idea it protected, creating space for further internal movement.

Our range of expression (where we can and cannot connect, what we allow ourselves to perceive or admit about ourselves and others, and our capacity to be intimate with the whole of reality) is determined by arbitrarily defined rules we have for ourselves and how rigid they are. The person with the fewest rules has the greatest capacity for love and insight.

Rules are upheld by judgment, and the judging mind is not permitted to see into the heart of things. Nothing that feels judged will reveal its essence, so while our rules may keep us feeling safe, it will be at the cost of removing us from the truth of reality. Though reality may seem to conform to our judgments, in the end we will always be betrayed—it is within all things where the perfect power of Eros is found.

An Erotic axiom: where an essence remains concealed, a rule is revealed. OM brings our rules to the surface so that we may examine them. Whenever we are judgmental, irritated, or withdrawn, one of our rules is being violated. Note that it is not us, the individual, who is being violated; it is our rule that is being violated.

When the world, in the form of our stroker or strokee, is refusing to conform to our internal rules, we have two options: we can break open the rule and receive the power the rule contains, or we can avoid it and lose an opportunity to realize.

We may have a rule about the speed, the pressure, or the attention of our partner. We may have a rule about the spot, or the way our partner should smell or not smell, look or not look. We may have a rule about the form the connection between us and our partner should take. We may have a rule about the sounds in the room or the sounds emanating from our partner. We may have a rule that they are supposed to compliment us, or not look at us. We may have a rule that says the felt experience of OM is supposed to be a particular flavor like deep and beautiful or gruff and earthy.

We are each an interconnected being with a unique expression, so any interior rule we break only breaks us open to a new facet of ourselves. Sooner or later, every rule we have will be brought to light in order to be dissolved by Eros (should we seize the opportunity), until at last we encounter the aspects of ourselves that cannot be dissolved. The Erotic self is indestructible.

Our experiences of OM and life are constantly informing each other through the lessons we learn in both. The moment we break a rule and receive more pressure than we would have asked for, we learn we are resilient. When we break a rule that the speed must be slow, we learn we have a capacity for flow. Likewise, the moment we break a rule around our partner having to pay attention, we learn that we ourselves can maintain the connection even when the other falters. We see the deeper truth that our rules, which we thought defined who we are, in fact limit how we see ourselves and what we are able to do.

5.
PLAYING WITH POWER

Working with Eros requires an approach that is diametrically opposed to the one we employ with the rational mind. With the rational mind, we seek to control; with Eros, we seek to live at the edge of our control, pushing our boundaries consistently. This is how we develop the skills that fill the gap between our current capacity and what draws us forward into the unknown.

True power is 360 degrees of power; it is the capacity to access power in all directions. All power is rooted in the body and in the deeper truth of our perfection.

If our actions are akin to a sword, the power behind the sword that gives us the capacity to wield it is our understanding of perfection. Perfection buys us time and space outside of the maelstrom of mind traffic, allowing us to gather ourselves and determine the precise action required while also always operating within the seamless connection of the whole. The power rises up in a particular form to act, think, and see in conjunction with all other aspects of reality. Power can also pull down and in, drawing forth our excess to empty what is full; or it can come from the other in order to expand what can flow between the two.

Power is the ability, in equal parts, to go and to stop. We go when we are called, stop when we might crash, and we sense the difference between the two beyond what our preferences might tell us.

When the mind is in service to the body and the body is in service to Eros, we become powered—the impersonal capacity to be operated through. As we inhale, we absorb tumescence and draw forth power. We use our attention like a sword to cut through tumescence. The power then becomes the breath, exhaling with agency. The Eros that lies within us is what converts and sends the energy back out, now purified as love.

When the mind is disconnected from the body and thus disconnected from the environment (in this case, our partner) one of two things occurs, likely in an alternating current. We experience a lack of power or powerlessness, and then to counter, we use force. Power would never use force because it knows it does not have to. Power understands that force will never yield erotically beneficial results for anybody. This is because it is action originating from the rational mind, which is disconnected from the whole by its nature. Force is an activity of disconnection and so carries out further disconnection. This includes "rationally good" activity. Power understands the recognition of our powerlessness is in fact the most powerful admission we can make.

Vital to note, however: true power may hurt. In our tumescent culture, we often conflate hurt and harm, which hinders true power.

Hurt is good and often the first step away from harm. Hurt is the experience of fixing a cavity, whereas harm is the choice to eat sugar and not care for our teeth. More often than not, we disallow the activities that would bring about the sword that cuts through tumescence, labeling them "harmful."

This single misunderstanding has astonishingly dangerous results. Tumescence is allowed to run rampant. We are rendered fragile and incapable servants to the ever-increasing demands of the discomforts of tumescence. Our capacity for resilience is inhibited. We become slaves to our attempts to decrease the intensity of life to accommodate our fragile, overly sensitive selves, rather than developing and unleashing the internal power that could meet life on its terms.

In OM, the phases of opening and turning on often involve some hurt. The process of life entering into something that has become numb or deadened is inherently uncomfortable. Ideas about ourselves that could only adhere to our identities in a state of low power have adhered nonetheless and must now be shed. This kind of pain is a touchstone when it comes to growing our power. We need to build a relationship with this kind of pain. If we don't, we will never open up and will consequently fail to grow.

We will instead spend our lives attempting to shelter ourselves from the discomforts of life, hunkered within our own bodies, demanding different circumstances and comforts. We will invariably be restricted to the bounds of a child's consciousness, as those who must be attended to and who require attention, rather than moving into an adulthood where we are the ones who can attend to and care for the uncomfortable. As Erotic adults, we can reverse the child's mind of rights and entitlements that aims to be seen or understood, loved or consoled, and instead be the vessel that offers such.

Erotic adulthood is the result of the inflowing of Erotic power that first fills us with love, understanding, and consolation. Erotic power doesn't come from the outside; it flows from within, giving us the resilience to face the pain of the world. When we are with others, we are able to carry out actions that cut through this pain. These actions are rooted in true power. We are not merely enabling or catering to the demands of another's pain; instead we are able to face the tumescence that holds the other person in its grip. We are able to operate with the courage that is required, a courage that demands power come through.

Power, with its inherent magnetism, is baffling to the rational mind because it does not understand that denial, ignorance, or saying that things are other than they are has no effect on power. Power is incorruptible. Power will continue to pull into its sphere what it hungers for, with or without the guiding assistance of the mind.

The juncture of power and words has other implications. When we are under the influence of our tumescence, we will act in opposition to power. We seek comfort and control in our attempt to craft reality around our tumescent expression, whatever it is. To the degree a strokee has realized her power, she can allow it to guide her through the OM and, by proxy, guide her partner. This is the true spirit of guidance in OM. When she allows her tumescence to guide, she is acting in opposition to power and will rely on the rational mind's sense of what treatment it can demand from reality, and again, by proxy, her stroker's body. This presents the stroker with an Erotic conundrum: if the stroker can sense that the guidance being received is veering the OM further into tumescent territory, any attempt to adjust the direction will fly in the face of that rational demand as essence will have been touched in spite of a rational rule. If the stroker does nothing, they will end up at the mercy of their partner's tumescence, which occurs in the reverse fashion: the rational mind of the strokee running over the Erotic sense of the stroker.

The neurosis women feel is the neurosis of tumescence when it is left undisturbed. The smog, confusion, pressure, and irritation a woman feels is the result of a buildup of tumescence. Tumescence makes others its enemy, which keeps her from the kind of contact that would switch on her power. This is why, in OM, a woman learns to use every ounce of her power to empower her stroker, making them powerful and strong as she sends them in to contend with her tumescence. She must look at what inside of her is making her feel disdain, disgust, and terror, and recognize it as the lens she sees life through.

When we dissolve our own tumescence, a miracle occurs. Much of what we consider outside of our preferences is often not only tolerable, but desirable. The strokee can respond to a variety of pressures, speeds, and directions without feeling harmed because they find within themselves the capacity to meet the stroke.

It is possible to entertain all the grievances tumescence might manufacture when threatened, allowing it every inch of its protest, while also remaining tethered to tumescence's deeper desire: to exhaust its various machinations and threats, and then be reabsorbed by the Erotic body.

This process is clearly not for the faint of heart. This is why at every point we need to have an escape hatch. One tool we can employ in the process of converting tumescence to power is a safe word. Pick a benign word such as "book," using it as a signal to stop or slow down. This enables the honest vocalization of tumescence to run itself out regardless of the form it takes.

Tumescence is wholly concerned with self-preservation, whatever the cost. Consequently, it tends to use words that would normally stop action. By using a safe word, our partner can be sure it is the tumescence and not us that is speaking. If we, the stroker or strokee, are truly in too much pain or need to stop, the agreed upon safe word is employed.

Each OM partner is instructed to remain rooted in the practices that keep them steeped in power. No matter what comes up during our experience, we then take the appropriate action. Instead of falling into reactivity, we allow the energy to run out by making decisions rooted in power. These rise up from our deep-seated sense that we are connected within a seamless whole. The world looks very different from this position.

Power, for the strokee, is the determination that there is absolutely nothing that would justify ejecting consciousness from the body. This is the secret. True power is the capacity to allow ourselves no excuse to leave the source of power, the capacity to say there is no possible version of ourselves that will make us leave our home under any condition. More importantly and more commonly, we stop seeking justifiable reasons to do so. Justification is how we build a rational case against reality, and nothing could be more dangerous to the Erotic self that wants to know reality in its true form. Nothing is heinous enough or attractive enough that we are willing to leave this body for, or that we need to avoid. Every individual has the power to stay with the body. When it is employed, the experience of harm, real or imagined, is greatly diminished.

To exercise our birthright of Erotic power is to determine that under no circumstances will we abandon ourselves. Whatever the culture says, there is never a justifiable reason. We determine not to opt out of our incarnated experience. This is a key characteristic of Erotic adulthood, the state of adulthood we may not have been able to touch until now. Hampered by the repressed Eros in the culture surrounding us, we were not aware of a power to work with.

A culture with no power is rife with ideas that never make it out of the realm of the theoretical, as there is a lack of power to carry them out in the material. Everything must be handled with kid gloves and legalism because, in a culture without Eros, we must prevent the spontaneity of truth that is in itself powerful and could "harm" those without power.

The human truth of hungers and drives and the impulse to feel our impact in the world are truths of an integrated humanity that cannot be permitted to come into plain view if people lack the power to face these truths. Consequently, they are driven underground, where they gain in power as we decrease in our capacity to meet them, until they explode, and our lives are shattered. At this point we can either wake up or be traumatized further as they eat us alive from the inside in the form of stress and tension.

Another reason we have issues with power is that we do not acknowledge the inward-facing form of power, the feminine form that draws in from the world like a magnet. Not acknowledging this form has made this kind of power dangerous. It is equivalent to determining that nuclear power is too much for humans to confront. Rather than learning more about this feminine form (how to use, direct, steer, and connect it to consciousness), we prefer to deny its existence in what amounts to massive cultural collusion.

This feminine form of power is the same force that turns birds in unison. When a child is pressed against an adult's chest, this power also causes the child's heartbeat to regulate itself with the adult's heartbeat. The same power draws a monkey two hundred miles when another is in estrus.

The beauty of this feminine form of power is that it can be made conscious and volitional. When it isn't conscious and volitional, this power can cause damage. When that happens, it seems like our lives are mysteriously happening to us. We cannot see, or won't admit, we have drawn to us precisely what our body was hungering for. This baffles the rational mind, which responds by ignoring it, believing this denial will stop the body from relentlessly pulling our hunger into the light of day. This is why it's crucial to understand that no amount of ignorance or denial is able to affect the pull of this incorruptible feminine power. With or without the guiding assistance of the mind, it will continue to pull whatever it hungers for into its sphere.

The mind believes if it can disconnect from its hunger, the hunger will go away. It will not; it simply continues to influence the world around the body without the cooperation of the mind. Peace occurs only when the two (mind and body) operate in concert. Otherwise, the mind tends to feel the body is sneaky, or even dangerous. It's up to the mind to determine the body is neither. But either way, the body will not be stopped or ignored.

The body contains a supernal calling within itself that it must follow with or without our permission. This is the truth we become progressively more cognizant of on the path of Eros. Our ability to perceive the invisible activity of the body is the difference between heaven and hell, or the difference between having superpowers or being controlled and manipulated by circumstance. This power cannot be corrupted, but with great love, care, and attention it can be guided into greater and greater efficacy of expression. When this expression of power is cultivated, it occurs as brilliance. When it lacks cultivation, it expresses as reactivity.

Each of us bears our own legacy of personal power. We cannot alter this. An inborn level of personal influence exists in each of us that is in accord with the calling on our heart. We can, in this lifetime, increase this sphere of power through OM and the careful and courageous unleashing of Eros into our systems. To the extent we do this in accord with the mind, it will manifest as the empowerment we have sought.

All empowerment is for one purpose: to share power. It may not be in a form others appreciate (we all have our own unique blueprint as to how it wants to be expressed), but it is always in connection and for the benefit of all, even if that means it hurts sometimes. If, however, we increase power beyond where we have cultivated the submission of the mind to the body, we will experience chaos and wreckage. We will be in overdrive without a steering wheel or brakes.

Three kinds of power exist: active, receptive, and transceiving. The latter allows us to live off the surplus power generated through connection. There is power in play. This expression of power is Eros-specific. It is power, and the expression of power. As it is liberated from need, power in play is rooted in optionality. It can go anywhere.

Just as we come to delight in our ability to hit the felt tone of a particular spot, especially when it was a spot that seemed out of range or unattractive, we become able to see how that note fits into the whole of the sensory music. We come to delight in our capacity to play in all of the dimensions of power with equal and simultaneous expression.

When a person who shuns expression can operate with equal facility in the overt as they do under the radar, this is true power. When a person who usually thrives in dominant or penetrating expression can learn to receive with a matched openness, this too is true power. When partners exist in perfect, complementary harmony across from each other atop a spinning ball and can take their respective power positions with equal skill, keeping the connection unbroken, this also is true power. Power is also the ability to eroticize any position we might find ourselves in, experiencing it as charged and alive. Even the position of powerlessness can bring with it tremendous and desirable arousal.

It is a law of power that the above is not truly above until it knows below equally well and can see, learn, and honor the power of *pull*. The converse is also true: the power of pull is of little use unless it can see, learn, and access the agency that can wield that power from within with precision, skill, and acumen.

When both powers come to know what it means to be the other, the age of Eros has arrived and the divine is awakened.

6.

AMBIVALENCE

When the *rational mind* is in charge, we consider ourselves successful when we corral reality over to one side and make a clear determination of whether that reality is black or white, good or bad. This is not true with Eros.

The signifier of life in Eros is the charge we experience, and for a charge to exist there must be ambivalence. We must have both lust and disgust, attraction and repulsion, desire and anxiety, because these poles travel together. The charge we experience is our opening to the fact that both poles are concurrently inside us.

Investing time and effort, we attempt to split the poles, and in the process end up splitting ourselves. We try to have only love and passion, only to discover that with time, dullness and hate appear. The practice of OM invites us to live in a reality where resolution can be achieved without exclusion of either pole. Resolution cannot arise from the security we experience when one of the poles is dead; it arises only when its complementary pole is present. OM invites us to grow enough to simultaneously encompass both poles.

It can feel uncomfortable to want and not want at the same time, or to feel both the heat and the cold that accompany a stroke. It can feel uncomfortable to want to pull in more sensation and to push the finger away, and then to open so that a third occurrence can happen. This third occurrence, which happens when we are able to hold a state of ambivalence, is always something new, something we have never known. The challenge now is that the poles are that much more powerful, so the attraction/repulsion factor is that much greater, and we have to expand that much more.

A charge inhabits our bodies. This is what makes us swell, and if it is not there, we are indifferent. Indifference is the purview of the rational mind, unless we find a way to eroticize indifference by adding in a counterpart pole to bring it alive. We will feel a warmth, along with a soft feeling of kindness and love. An intimacy with life begins to arise between the two.

Erotic ambivalence is the food of an Erotic life. In OM, we are either expanding our ability to contain opposites or, if we find single poles, searching for their complement. Good, as it turns out, is not good enough. We need to add in the richness and complexity of the bad. We can do the same with the beautiful, the imperfect, and the ugly. Countering poles add the charge that stirs and evokes sensation.

We don't play the instrument of our body in order to soothe ourselves and go to sleep. We play the instrument to awaken and sharpen the senses, to stir the depths of feeling wherein lies knowing, and, ultimately, to tap into the *sublime*.

7.
ANTICIPATION

In a goal-oriented world, the experience of anticipation is akin to torture. We have somewhere to go, somewhere to get to. The pressure builds within us, and we can't wait to exit into the relief of accomplishment. In Eros, it is the increasing of Erotic potential that allows us to expand and savor.

The rational mind sees the moment we presently find ourselves in as insufficient, always creating a goal to escape to something better. Because we already have such a buildup of undischarged tumescence, we feel like a pressure cooker; the thought of deliberately building sensation seems unbearable. To the rational mind, there is only one side to the pole, always wanting something other than what we already have.

In Eros, we are at home in the mind that approves of what is, and thus seated in the full, saturated perfection of this moment. The consideration to add more saturation, more concentration, to what is already perceived as good becomes desirable.

In Eros, we begin with *having*, so the perfect counterpart that adds the needed dynamic tension rather than mere intention is *wanting*. Few people have been trained to skillfully want: to reach for a stroke, to allow space for desire to build. We are so accustomed to a feeling of hypersensitivity that the moment real sensation starts to come alive, we experience it as uncomfortable and are inclined to rub it out.

We know how to consume ad infinitum in order to blot out the discomfort of all that our senses have consumed. To the overfull nervous system, any incoming sensation seems to knock up against the ceiling of what we can receive. But we do not know the true art of savoring, which is, in fact, the height of sensation.

The feeling of having is a part of *coming down* after expansion. We do not know how to do this well, and tend to skip over the integration that is part and parcel with having. We hunger, consume, and receive, but we do not acknowledge. As a result, we return to hungering.

In Eros, we learn to anticipate by savoring. We listen for the deep, rich chords of yearning. Rather than avoiding the gap between having and wanting, we make the gap our home. We discover that drawing our mind into this space brings us into the richest sensations of our experience.

In this gap, Eros opens to reveal the richness that lies in between, a richness that makes the flavor complex and opens us to abiding enjoyment rather than fleeting pleasure. In this gap resides the opposites. The in-between is bitter and sweet, pleasant and painful, full and wanting, alluring and eternally frustrating. This gap calls forth an aspect of ourselves that is able to fill the open space. That aspect is consciousness. Bringing in consciousness takes us into the undeniable totality of the whole, and not just the aspects we glamorize. In other words, anticipation expands us. We witness our relationship to the unknown manifest. The question is: do we meet the unknown with the anxiety of needing to know, or do we lead with our ignited potential, hungry to demonstrate our prowess?

We are seeing, at a deeper level, our relationship to power. Saturated with power, we know our resilience and our potential for recovery. We can afford to delight in the unknown—for it to develop our skills, to demonstrate our ability, and to face the inevitable failures that will grow us. As our experience in the gap teaches us, arousal is anxiety turned outward. When anxiety has pummeled us enough, we try something new, and the once-locked door of savoring opens.

Savoring brings us to an Erotic truth: not only will this life never be consummated where the gap between the self and the other is closed, we do not actually want it to be closed. It is only in this gap where dynamic aliveness is free to flow. We discover that what happens within this in-between place is what we have been looking for. What we desired was an excuse to draw us to where true desire exists. Once we are bathed in this truth, attainment of what drew us is of less importance, and enjoyment upon reception is that much greater.

THE FIVE CORNERSTONES OF ATTENTION

8.
THE CORNERSTONES

We want to learn how to work with Eros so we can restore agency at the deepest levels of cause and effect. Through the five cornerstones of attention (approval, intuition, power, intimacy, and optionality), we develop the skill to listen to Eros, recognize it, be with it, and be moved by it. Only then can we open ourselves up to the possibility of entering the *Erotic mind*.

Approval allows us to open to the totality of life. Intuition and power allow us to listen to Eros and develop the capacity to act on it. Intimacy and optionality enable us to experience moments in all their intricacy, making it possible for us to visit any location. Together the cornerstones help us cultivate a powerful, dynamic attention capable of operating at all levels of intensity and subtlety, in all conditions, allowing us to engage in the infinite play of life that is Eros.

Approval

Approval is the ability to see the full spectrum of life, the willingness to engage with it, and to love it no matter its content. Approval is admitting and looking directly at what is, without necessarily agreeing with it, and without attempting to bend it to our will.

When we meet an experience with approval, we choose a perception that seeks beauty and truth rather than judgment. Approval seeks truth over fear; it begins with the conception that this (whatever it is that life brings us in any moment) is right. The whole of life is right, and we need to discover how. Approval can turn a situation that is a potential threat into potential power.

Intuition

We develop intuition by learning to actively receive the directions we hear, no matter how subtle, nuanced, or mysterious they are. Reception is distinct from projection, as projection may include fantasy or imagination.

Fear and behaviors that are out of alignment with our deeper values cut us off from our intuition. When we are projecting, we cannot simultaneously be receiving. When we are passively receiving, information is filtered through default and preformed views. Intuiting Eros requires us to be prepared for the unknown. Relaxing into uncertainty, we listen with curiosity and are open to possibility.

Power

Power is the ability to stay conscious and maintain volition in the face of programmed behavior; it is the ability to use attention to organize and direct psychic energy. Power doesn't occur solely as defiance or rebellion, though defiance and rebellion can at times be part of its expression. Real power comes when we are able to change what is around us through our presence alone, and then make a choice as to whether we will be changed by the condition in which we find ourselves.

Intimacy

We explore intimacy through relationship with the things around us. When we allow ourselves to be permeable and accessible, we can enter other worlds and allow them to enter us. Intimacy is living in the reality of conversation with the whole of life—interior life, human life, wildlife—and the various expressions of the underlying force that inhabits all.

We can develop the ability to feel a moment in its full expression: tremulous or bright, strong or soft, vibratory or smooth. We learn how to be fully present, open, and engaged with our internal and external worlds. We feel and relate to anything and everything we experience. The empathy we feel when there is this resonance is intimacy, and we only ever harm that which we cannot feel.

Optionality

At the core of our being is optionality, a consciousness that allows us to go anywhere. Optionality provides access to all gifts—the full spectrum of potential where we feel most ourselves because every aspect of us knows it may be invited out at any moment. This is ultimately what we are seeking: a sense of everything being open and limitless. This is the home within ourselves to which we return.

From this location of optionality, every part of us becomes available. It is a dynamic state of consciousness where possibilities are numberless.

THE FIVE CONDITIONS

9.
INTRODUCTION TO THE FIVE CONDITIONS

Five conditions are necessary for Eros to fully connect with our being in a sustainable manner that brings about our full activation. This state is optionality, where Eros progressively increases in potency, and is dynamic and decentralized. In the absence of optionality, a contraction occurs as disassociation, impotence, fixity, and localization of experience. We call this contraction *deactivated Eros*.

While we cannot manufacture activation, we can set the conditions for it: safety, power, variety, connection, and extension. Having all five of these in place is similar to creating the conditions for a plant to grow: we don't need to force it, and we cannot guarantee the plant will grow, but when soil, sunlight, water, nutrients, and pruning are present, the blueprint that lies within the plant is activated.

Likewise, when the five conditions are present in us, our growth as individuals is activated. Just as a higher quality or lower quality of sunlight or soil affects how long a plant will grow, how quickly, and with what level of resilience, such is the case with these conditions.

We can access the five conditions artificially (meaning externally), or we can access them organically (meaning internally). For the most part, humans have been trained to access activation externally, and the results, while they may appear positive, are neither sustainable, resilient, adaptive, or fulfilling. The process of our practice is a progressive shift from reliance on external sources to reliance on our internal, organic resources to produce growth.

10.
EVOLVING SAFETY

Activation of the involuntary is key if Eros is to flow through our system. The only way for this to occur is relaxing or sinking into our bodies in this moment, right where we are; a letting go.

For this to happen, there must first be a fundamental feeling of safety. In OM, we progressively draw the locus of safety into ourselves, and as we do so, we become more virtuous. Erotic virtue is realized when the most potential for growth exists with the least amount of reliance on the environment. As our needs for safety are met more and more internally, we come to experience unconditional self-possession.

The six levels of safety:

1. We do not feel safe. We are frozen and cannot let go. Our heads are brimming with swirling, discursive thoughts that often take the form of judgment of ourselves and others. Hyperreactivity in the body occurs in the form of jumpiness or oversensitivity. We may attempt to create an inner sense of safety through disassociation, "checking out" through fantasy, or withdrawal of consciousness.

We may do this through an inner rejection of our experiences or through "pumping up" the positive aspects of experiences, overriding any feeling of lack.

2. We feel a tenuous safety through the means of deprivation and control within ourselves and externally. We attempt to control the environment

(the actions and activities of others, the strict adherence to protocols, the meeting of preferences) and ourselves through the immediate cessation of activity the moment a sense of violation occurs.

The externalized version of this behavior is a demand on our environment to decrease the level at which life expresses itself, and to do the same by suppressing the desire that seems to "just happen" to us. This behavior may be seen as equivalent to having an immune disorder and demanding that life sterilize itself through the assertion of rights and entitlements. This mindset, with its accompanying demands, often causes others to feel unsafe, yet it is so consumed with its own sense of danger that it does not notice.

At this level, we can instead move to a more internalized form of safety where we employ a container. This takes the form of an arrangement between willing participants to uphold a set of dependable agreements. In this way, the vigilant part of the mind can let go, knowing it is safe. And should the vigilant mind not feel safe, it has recourse in that we can always opt out. Within this container, we can grow our resilience and trust, thus attaining a deeper level of internalized safety.

3. Through practice, we have uncovered a basic sense of resilience. We have increased the capacity of the mind to meet circumstances, and in this meeting we discover that what seemed threatening was merely unfamiliar. We have increased our power and vitality by introducing more Eros into the body. Our baseline has moved to one of basic trust, and we are in the midst of moving our locus of trust into ourselves. In so doing, we discover it is a result of our trust in ourselves that we find a response, rather than placing the onus on the environment. But this sense is new, and the guide rails of the container are still required.

4. We feel fundamentally safe. Not only are we now able to explore within the rules of the container, we are able to explore the rules themselves—playing with them while maintaining connection with Eros, our partner, ourselves, and our environment. Practice takes on a more spontaneous quality in which we can go "off path" and riff, always coming back, when we venture too far, to the basic container and

protocols. We respect, depending on the practice, that leaving the container will often mean we are no longer participating in the practice itself, as is the case in OM, which is clearly defined and structured.

5. We have opened a gateway where safety takes on a whole new meaning. Safety no longer means self-preservation and survival, but is instead about remaining connected to the draw of Eros, no matter where Eros takes us or the intensity of the experience we find there. We have broken through a sound barrier. We are able to do things we might have once perceived as dangerous. But plugged into the force of Eros, we feel safer than we ever did in more controlled environments. A fear of loss and of threats falls away, replaced by a deeply rooted sense of calm and curiosity. What had before occurred as obstacles to safety, or as threats, now occur as opportunities to develop this powerful connection that confers the sensation of the only safety there is: presence.

Reaching this level of safety is a signifier that we will begin to naturally (not recklessly) move toward, rather than away from, what we once perceived as dangerous. In fact, the behavior we previously employed to feel safe is what now feels reckless, because it decreased our sensitivity to our environment.

6. We are now a source of sympathetic safety for others. We have converted so much fear to power that by not fearing what terrifies them, and by remaining open and emanating this power, we have a calm, stable field for them to tune into, should they choose to. We no longer resist fear but are now quite intimate with it, and can know and connect with people and life from these depths.

11.

EVOLVING POWER

True power is the experience of volition. Ultimate power is the power to choose to be with life exactly as life is. When we do this, we experience power as strength, a fundamental feeling of "rightness," vitality in the body, and the capacity to magnetize the world in a way that is congruent and harmonious with our deeper desires.

The four ways to access power:

1. We feel powerless because we feel life is happening *to* us. Caught in a trance of our own creation, we believe we have given our power to another person or experience. We alternate between feeling at the mercy of, or feeling as though we are being forced into doing something, so we fight, block, or dig in.

This feeling of powerlessness is the result of operating out of accord with a life that rewards by powering us. We demonstrate an unwillingness to make the descent into the body to break the spell and access our power. As a result, any descent or loss of control causes a collapse of consciousness.

2. Compensatory power is where we begin to activate power. However, compensatory power hasn't fully evolved; instead it's more a sensing of our impact. One of its primary expressions is commerce—we may feel powerful by withholding, causing another to suffer as a result. Women

often withhold sex, approval, and the emanation of turn-on from men. Men often withhold vulnerability and intimacy.

Compensatory power fails to acknowledge that all experience is shared experience. To acknowledge this would be a realization of true power wherein the rewards are intrinsic, meaning they are self-rewarding: nothing else is needed because the experience itself is whole and complete. Extrinsic rewards, on the other hand, are those that come from outside the experience, such as receiving a promotion and using that as a sign of power.

When we feel a lack of power, our bottom line is the question, "How will I get mine?" And the result is a power play or power struggle as we look for rewards outside of connection itself, without cultivating internal power.

With this mindset, we confuse power with authority. Power is a surge within the body that gives us the strength to carry out the wisdom that emanates from within it. Authority is the force the rational mind employs to carry out idea-based rules of consciousness in a manner disconnected from the body. Authority is therefore finite while true power is infinite.

In practice, we learn to open up to this raw power that, because of the circumstances of everyday life, can easily erode into excitement, anxiety, or fear—emotions that share the same energy, only laden with residue. In practice, we learn how to be with the raw form as a purifying force rather than as something that merely sustains our congestion.

3. Will to power is an aspect of power where raw power has been turned up beyond our capacity to steer it. Its aim isn't to get something, but it's a drive to express ourselves that has not been given the brakes.

This kind of power can be beautiful and dangerous. Will to power is a drive that causes us to create beyond what our bodies can withstand; it is behind much of what we know as great art or innovation. But without this power's full connection to a consciousness that can steer it, it can run over people and cause damage in situations where the pursuit overrides the needs of the moment. This is the result of consciousness not fully surrendering to the body, combined with the body's need to express itself. It is a "consciousness bypass" where the body resorts to going it alone when it feels our conscious mind would inhibit rather than contribute to our full expression.

4. Evolved power is an elegant system where consciousness makes the trek down into the body, fully hooks into its depths, and agrees to serve with its vision. This is where the vision and the capacity to steer and navigate with care from above are met with the drive for intimacy that would otherwise transgress boundaries. Consciousness adds a brake as well as a gas pedal to the experience of power, allowing us to use it with precision and resonance. Power can now be employed in its deepest realization: empowering others on their terms.

This is where we sense true unconditional power, the sense that no one is doing anything for or to anyone, only that this is what there is to do.

12.
EVOLVING CONNECTION

The state of Eros is fundamentally a feedback state of reciprocal and mutually influencing forces that together create a dynamic "third" energy composed of what exists between the connected two. True connection requires an intransitive consciousness that is dynamic, able to concurrently serve as subject and object. The healing we seek is found in connection itself, regardless of the outcome.

The four ways to access connection:

1. We feel disconnected. We know this because we have a feeling in the background that we don't belong, a scrambling to find connection at any expense, and a feeling of loneliness.

We might feel abandoned in some way, by something we may or may not be able to name. Since our system is open, if we are not careful, we will bond with anything to stop the smarting of disconnection—from people unavailable for connection, to food. In OM, we may bond with egoic arisings rather than with the actual connection that liberates. And until true desire is present, others cannot invite us into connection. Otherwise they will be doing so based on an idea conceived by the mind that doesn't represent the truth of the body.

2. We begin by connecting consciousness to the body. Until we do this, everything else we do is like attempting to fill a black hole: no matter what we put inside, nothing gratifies. This life-giving connection forms

the basis of goodness in our lives and, as a result, everything that occurs subsequently occurs as additive. We lack discernment until consciousness descends into the body. Our life, a sensing organ, will continuously seek outwardly, connecting randomly with people or things that will either harm or gratify it.

Without anything better to guide it, our sense of connection is driven more often than not by our history; we connect with things that resemble our past. This is entirely out of alignment with life's imperative to grow forward. This kind of connection is then a hindrance to growth. Instead of connection, we practice compliance, a performative way of acting how we think we must act in order for others to associate with us.

This performance kills all true connection because there is no way to perform while simultaneously connecting to essence. What we call connection is revealed as an exhausting form of pretending. Rather than seeking true connection, we employ all our power in pretending and may easily fall back into disconnection.

3. Through the safety and power we experience in OM, we connect to new sensations and experiences. We grow our depth of connection so that our intuition can show us what our overall system needs.

Do we feel full? Is it time to slow down or speed up? Are we gripping or holding on anywhere? Do we need to offer ourselves in some way? Because there are more options available to us, the feeling of disconnection begins to shift to a feeling of getting what we didn't even know we needed. We develop this capacity by adding power, helping us remain connected to everything we hear where we otherwise wouldn't have done so.

4. We are able to stay connected no matter what, serving as an outlet for others—especially those who could otherwise not connect out of fear they are dangerous or difficult to be connected to. We become a stabilizing force that changes the people around us, not by any effort but by being a place to connect. Through this, we naturally heal.

We witness in real time how pathology is the result of disconnection, and that nothing fancy or big is required in the healing of the world other than connecting to it.

13.

EVOLVING VARIETY

Untrained attention habituates to stimuli and as a result becomes passive. We can introduce variety as a way of keeping our attention active until it is strong enough to remain in a permanently active state.

The seven levels of variety:

1. We feel inattentive, dull, and bored. A quality of mundane repetition in life evokes a sense of being on autopilot. Life is drained of interest, meaning, and any sense of awe. We find ourselves waiting until the next experience catches our attention.

Increasing pressure, intensity, and drama are needed in order to attract our attention. We are unable to keep our attention on something without being distracted, and we are unable to lift our attention to focus on other things when we are done.

A pattern of stronger attention at the beginning is followed by diminishing returns. There is a charge when the attention has been "grabbed." We are looking to develop that level of charge in attention that, when evolved, is steady and continuous without either diminishing nor requiring external input to sustain. We may have settled into entirely passive attention that is low-grade and slack.

2. When desire breaks through this low-grade attention, it adds an active element to the mix. This active element will seek out novelty and

intensity as it is still somewhat weak but hungry. Led by a desire to consume experiences, people, places, and things, it will seek outside of itself.

A cycle of consumption occurs where something initially appears shiny. Then, the shininess diminishes until it no longer has power to hold our attention. It becomes a burden, an obligation, or something to be discarded. In this cycle, new input is constantly needed from the outside, only to be discarded later.

Many fail to realize the appearance of bright and shiny at the beginning is the experience of the attention being made active through novelty and then going passive as it lacks the "muscle" to hold itself up. The charge felt at the onset of something new can be indefinitely sustained, but not through external stimuli even when available in a constant stream of new and exciting. There will always be a rise, a peak, a diminishing, a cessation, and a seeking that will create an unstable attention accompanied by an underlying sense of desperation and fundamental insufficiency.

3. We can build our attention here in two ways. The first is to extend the enjoyment we experience with what we have, through digestion and acknowledgment. This shifts our attention from seeking to being, landing us in the present moment, which is where all gratification occurs.

The seeking mind, the mind that simply wants release, will run over the current experience with the desperation of someone who is starving—because the attention is, in fact, starving. The seeking mind lacks the capacity to metabolize and can only take in the quick hit of something new. Once we have settled into appreciating what we have through acknowledgment, we begin the next step of developing the subtle mind that is looking to feed on variety.

4. When we turn off the seek-and-consume mind and settle into a sense of basic sufficiency, we open a more nuanced form of noticing. Rather than needing the hard and dense experience of external reality, we begin to draw our attention to notice internal reality. We start with simply noticing the overall feeling in our body.

We notice the feeling of having our sitz bones on the chair, or the feeling of fabric on our skin. We notice sounds. We have downshifted from needing to draw in new experiences to finding newness in the experiences that are already here. The body feels a surge of power as the energy that was formerly expended on chasing experience is now able to stay in the body, helping the body meet its needs in the here and now.

5. We then dive further into ourselves, noticing our feelings. We allow our attention to move where there is a strong feeling or sensation. We feel for the heat, light, vibration, sharpness, or softness of it. As we focus, we notice whether it feels like we are descending or ascending. With something to focus on, our attention enlivens, now powered by the same energy that was formerly spent seeking. This yields a feeling of steady fulfillment.

6. We draw our attention even deeper into ourselves and notice more delicate nuances, the movements and rhythms of sensation. What happens when we move our attention from one location to the next? We will find that not only do external stimuli become less interesting, they become a distraction from the most interesting thing there is—this unceasing focus on the ocean of internal experience.

This is how our habit of external consumption falls away, and along with it goes the feeling of insufficiency. There is more than enough to keep the attention occupied with something that grows it, rather than erodes or merely manages it.

7. The final level of variety is marked by a steady sensation of gratification and little need for external stimuli. A permanent baseline of ambient attention is focused on sensation. The mind feels switched on as it is in the optimal position, open with curious interest in a way that it grows more complex and strengthens in the process.

14.

EVOLVING EXTENSION

Extension is the practice of expanding our homeostatic range. When done skillfully, this expansion increases our power and our uncertainty. We seek extension because it liberates our consciousness from habituated patterns that limit access to ourselves and calls forth greater resourcefulness, greater availability, and greater power from within. It sends signals that more is needed.

Extension sets a marker one step beyond the familiar, so close we must reach for it, while far enough that we become something more through our reaching.

The three levels of extension:

1. A mind that is not in perfect extension is either rigid with overextension or flaccid from a lack of extension (anxious or exhausted). It doesn't know how to locate the optimal spot where the mind is charged in perfect extension. It is either dragged forward by an idea that it should be more, do more, or have more, until it reaches overextension or collapses in on itself by the thought that it is not enough, it does not deserve, or it cannot succeed. It will ride these thoughts down until it reaches underextension.

People aim to have relaxed attention that is in a dynamic state of growth. Many have traditionally attempted to achieve this through external goals, competition, or working to be the best. The issue is this:

the monitor that can tell us what perfect extension is, is located within us. And these extrinsic ideas tend to have us overextend and experience burnout, injury, or a dissatisfying comedown on the back end.

In this cycle, we ramp up, enter overextension, then come down into underextension. The consciousness, while experiencing peak states, experiences them at a great cost. The alternative route involves never ramping up sufficiently to break through the wall of tumescence that occurs as resistance. Look for a spot in between where there is a consistent extension that cuts through tumescence without extending beyond where consciousness is able to go.

2. If there were only a single instruction, it would be to take a risk and stay with ourselves as we do. The issue with extension is that we get locked in a self-consciousness we cannot get beyond, so we bear down and "break through" just as we do with an induced climax. The only issue is that we break our connection to ourselves in the process, which occurs to the body as abandonment. The trick is to activate a constant attention that pushes forward without checking out. We must push to the very edge of where we can take our consciousness. If we are able to stay with ourselves, we must. But if we cannot stay with ourselves, we should not. This is the first stage. We would be wise to stay here until we break through the wall (and there is a wall).

At this edge, consistent repetition of activity will bring us to the wall and through it. Provided we move through the wall in what is called *perfect extension* (where we are pushing and relaxing at the limits of our skills and knowing), we will be able to maintain consciousness on the other side, which is important for sustainability. Otherwise, if we cannot maintain consciousness, a comedown with digestion will be required to enable us to return to consciousness.

As an alternative, we can remain with consciousness, but not in a way where we only allow limited stimuli rendering it lax, or in a way where we push beyond what we can move with. We aim for the sweet spot where we are pushing and allowing. This develops our consciousness through marathons rather than sprints.

3. As we adapt to this balance of consciousness, we notice extremes are absorbed into an expanding bandwidth. It isn't that our highs are not high or our lows are not low, but that they are contained within a larger consciousness and thus not experienced as extremes. It is the difference between an explosion happening underwater with the buffer of consciousness, or on land without anything to lessen the impact. This buffer optimizes the experience of growth, as what we learn is held in consciousness and our attention can let go and relax inside this larger field of awareness.

When we have this buffer, the body can release insight, intuition, and genius. These elements will no longer occur as explosions—flashes that move through us only to be lost. Any idea that comes to us can be caught and employed, implanted in an environment conducive to its gestation. Big moments of brilliance will not threaten the stability of the mind as it will have bandwidth for all of them. We discover genius is not the purview of the few, but is available to all who have expanded their field of awareness through regular, repetitive immersion in a field in which they push and relax concurrently. Having been so fortified, awareness is now able to receive genius, holding it in a way that, instead of destabilizing the mind, adds to its richness.

STROKING

THE SPOT

15.
THE CARTOGRAPHY OF THE CLITORIS

In the same way the language of paint is color and the language of music is sound, the language of intimate life is sensation.

Eros aims to draw us into the Mystery where the body serves as the medium between the forces of creativity and the instrument of our essence as humans. We can learn how to play and be played by these forces in elegant synchrony. We enter our training not as an aspiration, a duty, or a means of acquisition of greater awakening or the capacity to influence our environment; rather, we enter this training wholly as a labor of love. Our reward is the joy of being taken, drawn in, and informed by this intelligence in how to be evermore artfully expressed.

The marriage between a human being and an instrument creates music, whereas the marriage between a human being and the instrument of the body creates life. OM is the practice through which we awaken and liberate the artful sentience from within. This sensing force can hear, with acuity, the various notes of life and can respond with an elegance and uniqueness that expresses our essence in the world. Our essence is the unique sense of self that lies at the core of our interior that becomes activated in contact with the world of phenomena: eternal and unchanging, yet alive and dynamic.

Life through the art of OM then becomes a conversation flowing through us. Just as a musician hears the music within and allows their body to be transformed so it can come through, the OM practitioner listens to this sentience and attunes to it, allowing the body to become the instrument through which it plays into the world.

The aim is to be available for our unique expression, with acumen in all keys, tempos, rhythms, textures, harmonics, temperatures, and dynamisms. To be available is to be able to tune in and hear what wants to be expressed, to possess the technical skill to do so, and to have the finesse to bring it forward within the context of the existing sound of the world. We aim to play our instrument in collaboration with others inside the collective.

We are drawing forth the essential self from behind smokescreens and inauthentic presentations. This occurs as a kind of presence, and looks (from the outside) illuminated and radiant to the eye that can see. In the same way an artist cuts away stone that isn't part of the sculpture, OM cuts away from both partners whatever isn't part of the essential self or the genuine nature of their connection. The art of OM is this process of cutting away.

Just as we can understand art in theory but we cannot theoretically paint, dance, or sculpt, it's only in and through the instrument of the body that we can know our life at the level of Eros: the divine relationship between human and spirit that exists as creativity. We sink into our assignment as both created and creator; this is divinity not just in theory, but in practice.

In OM, at first it's quite likely that both clitoris and finger will occur, at best, as a fugue of sensations, with only a glimmer of hope of finding any one spot to turn on. But as we continue, spots begin to reveal themselves as worlds unto themselves, distinct with their own notes and flavors. Dimensions within the body can become whole practices in themselves. For instance, one could have a lifetime of rewarding experience solely by focusing on the nuances of the one o'clock spot. The mind could be trained to surrender to the body through this spot alone.

Ultimately, we are aiming for equal facility in each spot, forming a 360-degree consciousness that can enter and register all of the notes life offers. This translates into the capacity to experience the endless variety and beauty in all things.

OM has ten descriptive parameters: spot, lighting, stage, tempo, pressure, direction, texture, temperature, length, and harmony. Each parameter holds a dimension that allows an OM to be described. Because we are learning to draw the ineffable into our everyday experience, it helps to have categories to anchor our experience—specific ways to point to aspects that distinguish sensation. We build this sensory vocabulary in order to internally note these aspects for ourselves as well as communicate them to a partner.

Applying language to felt experience brings a tangibility that, in turn, allows for evolution. We begin to have the ability to track experience and draw it down from the mere ephemeral into the sensorially practical in order to relate with, grow, and attune to its various elements.

This is why we describe OM in terms of the descriptive parameters.

Lighting

Each variation of a stroke is like a filter for the lighting. We sense a perfect match for the "mood" of the spot. Just as we sense, according to our mood, whether we want a bright, open, sunny room or a dimly lit, warm room, each spot has a mood, and we can tell whether we are stroking with a matched attention based on whether the lighting matches. This is an example of resonance.

We observe this as a turning-up or turning-down of the brightness inside the mind's eye. We can also gauge it by its vividness and concentration. All matched lighting feels good, but as we develop greater sensitivity, it becomes more and more concentrated, as if its fidelity were increasing. This feels like a richness, a saturation. Finally we find a perfect focus. We all have a sense of what the right focus is; as the saturation of light increases and decreases, we will know when we have reached the right focus, because everything becomes clear.

We are looking for saturation as opposed to diffuseness. This requires a stability of attention so we can remain with the stroke exactly as it is. Otherwise, diffuseness or flickering of different levels of brightness translates in the body as agitation. We are looking for a continuity in the way the lighting shifts where it moves with the stroke as if it were on a dimmer switch being moved by a skillful hand that perfectly matches the internal mood.

We are also looking for the optimal range of brightness. If the light is dimmer than what feels optimal, this signifies attention has been withdrawn; if it is brighter than optimal, this indicates we are using our will. The optimal location is where the attention is resting in the body with optimal continuity—flexible, effortless, stable, and strong.

The Spots

Imagine the clitoris is the clock. The twelve o'clock position is the center, and the one o'clock position is on the strokee's left, if she were to look down, continuing down toward six o'clock at the bottommost position, and then back up around to her right.

Here are the primary spots and their locations. Through resonance, we can tell which spot is open and attuned, which is exaggerated, which is open and out of tune (i.e., filled with concepts), which is underexpressed, and which is not yet open.

The Home Spot: One O'clock

The one o'clock spot is the spot set by biology as the default setting for a universal *home spot*. A home spot is where the attention can naturally rest and where, when contact is made, an electricity begins to fill each partner.

For those beginning in OM, this spot is where sensation is coiled and progressively opens with the heat of contact. Resonance found in this spot can be sensed at first as a tiny buzz, similar to what we feel if a copper penny touches our tongue—a slight zing. As the spot opens, this buzz becomes more of a hum, eventually translating into a warm pocket where the attention can rest.

The one o'clock spot is where we practice "scales." Scales in OM involve direction, speed, and pressure. We work here to develop an attention that is tuned in, strong enough to cut through tumescence, subtle enough to note changes, agile enough to move through the changes, and steady enough to remain with each stroke without hovering or pressing in. We can think of our attention as fingers moving over the keys of sensation. The one o'clock spot is where we train the fingers again and again to collect information and express with fluidity.

An exaggerated response on the one o'clock spot suggests a striving in terms of sensation; at the most basic level, we "think" sensation in the mind rather than surrendering to it in the body, and we try to "pump it up" with performance-based expression rather than reception-based allowing. This kind of an exaggerated response is marked by a tension in the body coupled with driving at the point of contact, moving the body toward or away from the finger or clitoris rather than allowing either to be moved as a Ouija board planchette is moved. The lighting is normal room lighting.

Under-responsiveness suggests a kind of withdrawal of attention that scatters after being unable to connect to the electricity in the contact between finger and clitoris. Were contact to be made, electricity would flow through the connection and the line would go taut; with under-responsiveness, the line goes lax. There is not enough concentration of attention to feed the perception that would register the stroke.

There is also an actual, physical retreat of the clitoris, accompanied by an abundance of discursive thought often in the form of frustration, grief, a general sense of being lost or confused. The body has a deadened or numb quality where the clitoris may retreat or the finger may have no life in it.

VERTICAL SPOTS

The Spiritual Spot: Twelve O'clock

The spiritual spot (and its complement, the feminine spot) exists in the vertical with a sense of levity and liftoff, of leaving the laws of gravity. The mind has a pristine, empty, spacious sense marked by a feeling of breath and opening. As the spot is stroked, this high, open feeling reaches through the center of the body and opens all the way through the top of the head. We feel a profound sense of clarity.

When we feel a full twelve o'clock response, we see a kind of beauty and order to the mystery of sensation. We have a sense there is *only this*, that we have broken away from the illusion of anything else. The lighting ranges from bright to whiteout.

An exaggerated twelve o'clock spot will have a fussiness or preciousness to it that occurs as restlessness and control. A mental fixation on a certain state occurs over what is happening in the body. The mind can easily become fixated in such a state, employing an aggressive or demanding quality that orders the body to get it "just right" so the mind can get its fix, either of spaciousness or silence.

An under-responding twelve o'clock spot occurs as exasperation and a sense of meaninglessness, an impatience at having to "put up with this," a feeling of merely enduring what's happening.

The Feminine Spot: Six O'clock

The complement to the spiritual spot, the feminine spot is still on the vertical and is deep, rich, and nourishing. Here the body occurs as a refuge where bone and sinew ground and comfort consciousness while it descends into a deeper sense of knowing, healing, and power from below.

In the depths of the six o'clock spot lies a dimension of unique knowing, access to vision, and connection with the force of what we would call genius. The lighting ranges from dim and rich to blackout. One feels submerged in depths that cleanse and hydrate. A slowness to this spot is akin to moving in the deep aquatic, accompanied by a dissolution of boundaries. The spot, however, is clear, vibrant, and concentrated, like a well-struck note from a lower register.

An exaggerated state occurs here as a demand to stay out of control or as the quality of addiction; a refusal to be moved back into the boundaries of this world. There is either an over-stroking or a gravitational pull to continue stroking beyond the point the peak shifts. At this point, the mind then has the experience of drowning and becoming muddied; the mind pulls all resources into itself, and a feeling arises that the mind cannot be gratified under any circumstances. This translates into a state of desperation.

An under-responsive state means this spot has not opened; it occurs as a sense of dryness. The mind cannot properly attune so the activity in this spot becomes mechanical. It may note the direction, pressure, or speed, but it cannot feel or be moved by this sensation. Overall, the OM lacks the dimension of richness.

HORIZONTAL SPOTS

The Identity Spot: Three O'clock

When turned on, this spot is how the union between twelve and six o'clock expresses itself outwardly through the heart of a woman. An open, non-identified type of love issues from this spot. For each woman, the way she is meant to express love at the level of essence can be felt here. This love may be fierce, or may be gentle, nurturing, and inspiring; it will be felt in the bodies of both partners as the point of contact and draws down the potential of who they are as a whole, as love tends to do. There will be a sense of familiarity, akin to remembering oneself, or there may be a sense of settling into oneself, together with an ability to maneuver with grace.

Remember that the opening of this spot is directly proportional to the opening of the twelve and six o'clock spots. Its opening results from the other two spots opening and being connected. If they are not both connected, this spot will not switch on.

The lighting of the three o'clock spot is unique to the expression of each individual.

An exaggerated three o'clock spot occurs as an excited or dramatic expression. The sensation has a mania to it, even though it may not be apparent on the surface. We are performing Eros, perhaps adding in a sexuality or an innocence in order to get a result.

Under-responsiveness involves a belief that who we are will not be acceptable in the world. It can also indicate that a connection between twelve and six o'clock has not been made. We feel a sense of not being able to express or let out what wants to flow from us, as though we are backed up and stuck behind an invisible gate.

The Shadow Spot: Nine O'clock

The shadow spot is the spot that, when opened, allows us to access the sensations we may, for a variety of reasons, block. We may block our vulnerability in order to avoid being hurt, or we may block our hunger because we think we are too much. We may block ruthlessness or submission.

But when the shadow spot is stroked and opened, these sensations can flow and be integrated into the whole of our internal Eros at the level of sensation prior to thought. There is a sense of filling up an aspect of ourselves we didn't previously know was empty. A feeling that we did not know we were missing something and were not feeling gratified. The lighting of the shadow spot is often deep and rich, the way a room lit only by candlelight looks.

When this spot is exaggerated, we experience a fixation on a certain repressed aspect of Erotic expression, followed by a grasping for the same, singular aspect. While providing us with no sensation, such a feeling keeps calling to be stroked.

Under-responsiveness is characterized by an overactive twelve o'clock spot, which restricts and suppresses sensations so they cannot rise to the surface. The underlying sense is that we are potentially dangerous and must be scrutinized at all times. In the under-responsive expression, when there is any activation in this spot, we experience a sense of panic.

COROLLARY SPOTS

Relaxation Spot

Each woman and each clitoris has something new to reveal in terms of sensation. In addition to the more common spots described previously, there are a few variations. The first is the relaxation spot that resides just above the six o'clock spot, at the base of the ridge on the clitoris.

The feeling conferred when stroking this spot is that of a deep exhale. It's the perfect spot to stroke when anxiety is present. The relaxation we sense when this spot is stroked lies partway between the two extremes of sleep and anxiety—the pure opening of the body where we are awake but our mind is submerged. We are able to receive the input of stimuli through an open, whole sensory experience. Sounds become fluid, as if in a soundscape. The sights of the interior world recede. A beautiful hum or buzz spreads across the whole of the body.

In the exaggerated form of the relaxation spot, the mind is submerged so deeply it's as if we are in a dream and cannot awaken. There is a feeling that the mind and body have snapped apart and that the mind is drowning in a state of disassociation bordering on oblivion. The lighting is the warm, electric blue of dusk.

In an under-responsive state, we experience anxiety. If the spot is closed when the relaxation spot is stroked, there is an increased sense of mental chatter as well as a feeling of impatience.

Uplifting Spot

This spot is located on the ridge of the clitoris beneath the twelve o'clock spot. There is the sensation of reverence, with the attention reaching upward—almost a holding of the breath.

This reaching or yearning is mostly enjoyable: it feels like a good stretch for the spirit. The lighting is bright and the primary feeling is concentration that offers a deep sense of beauty. There is an added dimension to feeling akin to the quality of skin against skin or pure beauty or the sound of the breath. The simple is elevated to the profound and there is the feeling that it has always been there but this spot just needed to be turned on to sense it. The lighting is like a sunrise.

In its exaggerated form, an unintegrated or a dramatized expression occurs, carrying with it a sense that we are in the presence of something beautiful that will neither penetrate nor permeate us. We sense that to bridge the gap between receiving it and being moved by it, reverence must be performed.

An under-responsive state is marked by blankness as far as sensation is concerned, with neither irritation nor yearning present. There is quite literally nothing. The finger occurs on the clitoris as entirely physical with no dimension.

The "In Love" Spot

The "in love" spot is in the pocket back behind the two o'clock spot. This spot is marked by a feeling of arousal that wants to attach to something. When it's permitted to simply be open, there is a feeling of being a little in love with everything.

The feeling becomes nonlocalized and moves from finger to heart to thighs to the interior view. The mind is permitted to fall in love with all of it. There is a feeling that this essence is permitted to do what it most wants to do, and that falling in love with a person is only an analogue for the deep, abiding passion that wants to be felt in itself and not locked onto something. When sensed, this passion is radically deepening and regenerating. The lighting of the "in love" spot is warm, mid-level lighting.

The exaggerated form fixates and locks onto something, often on the practice partner. There is then an exaggeration of the appearance of romance or seduction that is performed.

In its under-responsive form, there is an overt feeling of blocking or rejecting as well as a sense of self-protection. One or both partners feels a prickly, almost barbed wire sensation.

Flavor

The flavor of an OM describes the primary dimension the OM occurred in. This corresponds to the spots on the clitoris that were the most lit up, and where they are located.

Stroking Suggestions

If a spot is not open, a good option is always to push out slightly. We underscore *slightly*—it should feel as if the finger or clitoris is exhaling. Sometimes this movement alone is enough to open the line for connection to run through.

The tendency with heightened sensation or speed can be either to clench against it or not to allow it to register, which means we disassociate or ignore it. Slightly pushing out draws the attention back to the point of connection. This helps to distribute sensation throughout the whole of the body, instead of allowing sensation to collect at the gateway of connection, where it can become backed up.

With a medium-speed stroke, a partner's attention may go lax, a result of feeling the situation is safe, without a need to pay attention. The key in this case is to move along with the strokee; this enables both partners to match the other perfectly, and brings attention into lockstep with sensation. This connection keeps it alive.

Slow speeds can allow aversion or irritation to set in. The body may feel like it's "revving," especially if it's fixated on climaxing—or the body may feel "stuck in traffic." The instruction here is to draw in the stroke the way we might draw in a beautiful view with the eye. This slows the revved attention and allows it to again rest purely within the sensation itself.

How we hold attention is not unlike how a master singer utilizes a microphone. Sometimes sensation is belted out, while other times it may be more like a whisper. The key is to maintain a continuous "sound" by adjusting our attention. This way, our interior self never has to strain to hear the sensation nor feel a shock at its intensity.

When attention is moved in proper proximity to sensation, we find the continuity we seek. Lacking proximal facility with our attention, we try to find it by tuning out or over-pumping in order to create the "perfect cocktail" of sensation. When we have facility, the continuity feels alive, dynamic, and concurrently still.

16.
JUST THIS STROKE

As hard as it may be for our overstimulated minds to believe, there is more sensation in any one stroke than almost any mind can fully receive. Our minds are so full that they cannot take much life in and, as a way of compensating, continue to ingest.

The solution to this type of sensory starvation—which drives rejection, grasping, and checking out—is to learn to "taste this bite," to feel this stroke, just as it is. This is a fundamentally different approach from the type of poor sensory nourishment we experience when we are both stuffed and starving because our calories are sensory-empty.

This state may occur as a blank wall of sensation. Here, we start by finding one thing—anything—we can sense, good or bad. We may notice a buzz, or a feeling of heat, or a sharpness, or a brightness. We allow our attention to connect with whatever we notice, and when we do, we discover that whatever we place our attention on grows.

To merely sense is challenging at first. A flood of judgments will want to enter and drown out the sensation; the key is to continue to return to the sensation. If we have to track this mentally—hot, soft, dark, electric—then we should do so. Continue to collect the attention there. We are communicating with our body, perhaps for the first time, showing it what it has to say is important, we are willing to learn its language, and we won't tune it out. We are willing to learn, sensory note by sensory note, until we have a full sensory vocabulary, until we become fluent, and then until we can communicate in the poetry or music of the body.

It all starts with this stroke. Everyone has at least one sensation that they can tune in to. The mind will want to continue its oblivion, like hearing a foreign language in the background that would take too much effort to tune in to. Still, we continue to immerse ourselves in the conversation and turn up our listening. All we need is one spark of sensation to build an entire Erotic mind.

We notice a magnetism to the sensation, and that there is a way we can move the mind to where it either fades or deepens. As we continue moving to where it deepens in each moment and with each stroke, the connection becomes stronger. The power pulsing through the connection between the spot and the mind grows clearer, burning off any debris in the line.

This is all we do: find a spot of sensation, note where it gets stronger and where it fades, then move toward where it gets stronger. It is never more complex or nuanced than that. Through this process, the mind becomes trained to follow sensation and, in turn, to follow Erotic truth. This will lead to greater intimacy.

17.
FINDING THE SPOT

The first step in connecting to the spot is remembering there is a spot. The spot is the feeling of direct experience, the state that exists beneath our fundamental confusion between who we are and what we do.

First, we notice. Do not take action. Simply rest the attention on the point of contact. We can't do this by force, but only by allowing our sensing to guide us as we seek to learn its ways.

If we are the stroker, we notice the sensation in our fingertip. If we are the strokee, we pay attention to our clitoris. We connect to what we feel. If we are the stroker, we keep our eyes open and our stroking hand relaxed—engaged but rested, as if gathering energy before throwing a ball.

When the finger touches the clitoris, both partners may feel an initial spark or buzzing. As the stroker, we notice whether our finger feels heat or vibration. We follow this feeling, letting it guide us. As the strokee, we allow our attention to become fluid, as if music were washing over us. We relax our body, especially our hips. We let our words guide the finger to our clitoris instead of extending our clitoris toward the finger. As the stroking continues and the finger draws closer to the spot, vibration and heat may increase. We may also notice a slight repulsion, almost pushing the finger away. When we feel this, we can lighten the stroke. Now, we may feel the finger being pulled in closer. Here, let the finger move only if it is being moved. The use of force to either move the finger closer or faster may cause the spot to close.

This is where having any sort of agenda may cause us to stiffen our senses, which stiffens the finger or clitoris and pushes the spot away. This is why goallessness is a defining aspect of OM. If we allow goals to get in the way of desire, the ego—operating through our thoughts—will outcompete it. Rather than attempt to stop our thinking, we can instead let thoughts just be thoughts and let our feelings be feelings, returning our attention to sensation. Our felt sense can bring us to direct experience.

When the finger first lands on the spot, we may feel that initial buzz enter our whole body. This means we are on the spot. The energy will increase and may lead to a homeostatic response, in which case our body and mind have sensed a change in their energy levels and will want to return to the familiar, the way a rubber band contracts to return to its unstretched state. This response is a kind of self-protection, and in the body it may take the form of a stiffening or bracing.

The mind, unsure of what is happening, may respond with fear or confusion, fantasy or greediness. Because it is particularly sensitive to the discomfort that results from influxes of energy, the mind will try to disconnect. The key is to stay connected by keeping our attention active, one stroke at a time; this inhibits the homeostatic response.

As the stroker, it's important to keep our attention focused on opening and allowing energy to move through us—as if the finger were inhaling. Connect to the sensation and draw it into the body. Eros lives in the dynamic tension between control and being out of control. Our ability to stay connected lives in that sweet spot, where we give up total control but retain control of our own experience through attention.

As the strokee, we will likely have a tendency to pull back or withdraw our attention. When this happens it has the effect of drawing the finger in too much and will feel as though we are being poked. Instead, we can allow our attention to open. Conversely, there is a tendency to reach out for the finger, but reaching out is also a kind of contraction of attention, a hyper-focus on the finger. In this situation, reaching out has the effect of shutting off the sensation. Instead, again, we allow our attention to become more fluid and open.

When we are on the spot, we feel everything. As the stroke comes fully into the spot, it may feel like everything suddenly drops away and becomes quiet. All mental chatter and physical discomfort vanishes. There is no more motion. We feel an electromagnetic hum that begins in the clitoris and moves over the whole body. We aim to make our finger an exquisite sensor and our clitoris exquisitely sensed.

When we get on the spot, there is a dynamic quality to the impact we have on each other. Each person impacts the other with subtle openings and closings. This is what Eros trains us for: the world of connection where the possibility exists for a feedback loop of mutually influencing systems. In OM, we can experience and acknowledge directly that we profoundly affect each other, that we can move and be moved with gentleness and build something together.

As we stroke the spot, we may feel as if our finger is being suctioned, that it feels locked onto the spot. It may feel like a current is moving up and through us. If we begin shaking, relax and allow it to move through the body; stiffening will only take us off the spot. We can stay connected by drawing the sensation up, remaining fluid, and allowing our finger to remain open. This may feel messy, but it allows us to feel each other as the sensation moves back and forth.

If we begin shaking or trembling, know that while it is not a problem, it may be a sign that a feeling has become stuck. Again, we need to pull it up from the point of contact and down into our body to ground it. Allow it to cycle all the way back down to the thumb and introitus. This cycling of energy forms a circuit through which we can build and release energy. To avoid contraction, we keep active, gentle attention on both the sensation and the connection. We know we are leaning in when we have a steady, continuous hum in our body and finger. This is the sensation of being "on." We feel the hum even in the mind.

As the strokee, we lean our attention in and allow the connection to move through us. When the stroker moves with our spot, there is an interior feeling like swaying in unison with music. We progressively feel more liquid, as though the finger is moving through a pool; what started as a distinct physical sensation, pressure, or heat now occurs as waves. Sensation is the music the instrument of the strokee and the stroking of the stroker make together. The sensation is both made by and develops the attention. The finger and the clitoris are both extensions of our attention, each contributing to the opening of the mind.

The aim is to stay connected. If our attention is distracted, the clitoris and finger will follow suit. What we want to develop is the kind of surgical attention that's strong enough to cut through bone—including all the sediment of thought, doubt, delusion, and fantasy—while cutting gently enough to operate at the microscopic level, and steadily enough to make a clean cut.

HOW TO STROKE

18.
LIFE IS AN OM

What we see in an OM is what we see in life. The exact same tendencies play out in endless varieties.

The mind is employed in the discovery of how to meet each experience. Where the attention might otherwise have gone into discursive thought, it's now aimed in the incentivized and unified direction of learning how to use attention to—almost like a musician—"hit the perfect note" that opens the field of awareness into the experience of the Erotic state.

We are always playing with the various rhythms, tempos, pressures, and notes of life. We do this not to be good but to be beautiful, to get to play our unique art across the entire spectrum of our life.

This is one of the beauties of OM. It recognizes there are universal rules we must play by for the activity of awareness to have the quality of art and neither be completely chaotic nor rigidly formulaic. OM asks for the unique, particular expressions of who we are, which each person alone possesses the capacity to unveil for themselves and then contribute. Our task is to find what unites all things, and then express from this knowing in a manner that is uniquely our own.

We start by learning the basics. We master the rules. We play inside the rules. After a time, with the entire palate of human sensory experience to draw from, we step into the art for ourselves. We are not reduced to the few default sensations of everyday life—fear, anger, excitement, and sadness. Instead, we develop nuance and subtlety, richness and depth.

Our perceptions aren't inextricably linked to circumstances, and our resulting interpretations aren't imprisoned by limited notions that fall into the domain of good versus bad, right versus wrong. Those kinds of notions play out when we are bound to the rational world of science rather than to the Erotic world of art. When we choose art, science is also available, but because science deals with the rational and the finite, it cannot encompass art.

In OM, we can develop masterful technique, superb proficiency, and skill. This mastery may take a decade or more, and equates to opening all spots, directions, speeds, and pressures, while developing an intuitive response in how to meet them. This is the launching point for the deeper experience—because the rules are now ingrained in our bones, we can venture out and play with them, just as a master musician plays with notes. We discover who we are and what we are capable of, not in theory but in practice.

We are able to know the edges of our sensory capacity and create unique compositions of sensory experience. We meet our partner in the field of intimacy but instead of either resisting the current or rowing with it, we launch a sail and go in any direction we wish, knowing the laws of motion and harnessing the intelligence of nature.

It all starts with a single stroke. Giving ourselves to the stroke that is here right now is the highest level of mastery.

19.
INTIMACY SPEAKS TO US IN SENSATION

We ultimately seek four things in life: to love and be loved, to see and be seen, to know our purpose, and to feel connection. We are drawn to the Erotic because we sense these things are possible through it. Sensation is the language through which these essential elements of intimacy are communicated; we know when they happen because we can feel them in our body.

We may have these kinds of experiences in OM. An OM can go from soaring and uplifting, to soft and dark, to outwardly expressive. We feel a vibration start in the other person's body and then run into ours. We notice a heat, and as we move into or away from this heat, the shakiness in our body increases or decreases. That is connection.

How do we get back to these resonant moments of sight, love, connection, and purpose as they are communicated by sensation in the body? How do we live our life inside these experiences? The way forward isn't scientific, and it isn't random; it is somewhere in between—an art.

In OM, beauty arrives through feeling. To be able to feel is the essential skill of Eros. Our attention must be so attuned because the beauty of OM is the emergence of the hidden self: the essential daimonic self that expresses, feels, and acts from our deepest involuntary nature. In OM and in life, we guard this essential self.

The work of OM is to draw out this essential self through its layers of protection. These layers are often the product of survival skills that evolved to help us navigate the vagaries of the world as we sought to feed our loved ones and ourselves. In order to reach beyond these layers and touch the truth, we must be willing to use our felt sense to guide us.

As a stroker, to reach a strokee effectively, we need to know the truth beyond what even she knows. We need to sense her beyond what even she is aware of sensing, beyond the smoke screens she may send—like when she rewards us for stroking the wrong location or utilizes added electricity to "turn on" a spot that isn't her natural spot.

We can learn to perceive when the essential self is emerging. The skill we are tapping into is a primitive skill, not a developed skill. We look for a concentration, like the foreground standing out from the background in an overexposed photo. We watch for changes in lighting because they will bring out the contrast, helping us to see. In OM, each stroke acts like a filter on this lighting. We are looking for where the lighting gets brighter or dimmer, more wavering or more stable, whether the sensation is closer to us or farther away. All of this tells us what is happening as Eros passes through us as we OM.

Optimal lighting has a certain concentration. Notice when the light becomes dense rather than diffuse. See if there is a continuity and steadiness rather than a flickering; where the light is neither too bright—where the attention is pushing—nor too dim—where the attention has been withdrawn. The optimal light is where the attention is stable and there is a continuity to the flow of Eros. It is effortless, easeful, flexible, soft, pliable, and can be moved. To find the optimal lighting, vary the location, speed, pressure, length, and direction of the stroke. The variety of sensations, the boundaries of those sensations, and the interplay between them elicited by any stroke indicate where Eros expresses. Different sensations can be grouped together, like different feeling groups that get played on the clitoris, including basic notes, primary notes, and the musical notes we learn to recognize and express in unison.

20.
FAST STROKES

While some use OM to add comfort to their already tumesced state, others choose the almost certainly uncomfortable experience of entering the Erotic body. These are entirely different orders of experience. In an OM, the amount of speed we employ will determine whether or not we are able to penetrate tumescence and enter the Erotic body. We must be clear with our partner on what type of OM we are looking to have, as the instructions around the usage of speed are quite different based on the intention. It is wise and practical for OM partners to share their intentions for their practice before beginning the OM and to get explicit permission if the intention and desire is to penetrate the tumescence, even with potential discomfort.

The truth about speed is that, without a fast stroke, there is minimal chance of breaking through the wall of tumescence most women live inside. The strokee's tumescence acts as a kind of brake. Having taken on a life of its own, the tumescence may throw up an automated protest by withholding, withdrawing, or venting aggression.

Using speed is paradoxical. Some strokers want to stroke fast but without consciousness. Because the role of the stroker inherently involves agency, these kinds of strokes support the stroker's form of tumescence where the drive to produce overpowers their ability to stay connected to what they are feeling. Some strokees want slow and conscious strokes, which support their form of tumescence.

A stroke that is both fast and conscious will challenge the stroker and the strokee in perfectly complementary ways.

To the extent that a woman is locked behind tumescence, the complementary energetic pole in her stroker will want to go harder and faster. She literally draws this urge from the other person. The challenge is that speed and pressure can only be done well with consciousness, but we tend to go unconscious as they increase. For this reason, the speed required to get through the tumescent sound barrier of an OM is rarely achieved.

Behind the scenes, while there is an under-the-radar call for a certain speed and pressure coming from the strokee, commonly there is also a hypervigilance around safety. The strokee has locked down her system because she feels fundamentally unsafe in life, and the power she would need to feel resilient and safe cannot flow without the speed that will bypass her vigilance: a double bind.

A few options exist. The strokee can commit to speed prior to the OM. The stroker can then use speed as a tool. However, the stroker must employ precise attention on every stroke. Like takeoff with an airplane, it's that much more important to pay attention. Planes crash more frequently during takeoff or landing.

More importantly, the stroker and strokee must together commit to the speed. This is the difference between a smooth takeoff and crashing into a wall. If she gave her stroker permission to use speed before starting the OM, the strokee will feel she can let go into the speed as it takes her where she could not take herself—through the gates of her tumescence. Life will have called her to speed up many times and each time she will have slammed on the brakes in protest. But avoidance can only delay this inevitable encounter. She will be sitting on a brimming powder keg of backed-up protest that will need to be exhausted. If she decides to explore speed all the way, she will be breaking through all of her fears and built-up resentments—all the places she was unwilling to meet life on its terms. These are what she is locked behind.

Just as she can sense when her stroker is unconsciously employing speed, if she senses the stroker is hesitant or fearful, they will be implicitly communicating there is reason to be afraid. We cannot ignore this level of communication in an OM. In fact, it is at this level that most communication happens. She is sinking into her power, her deepest knowing that the world is safe as she breaks through a tumescent trance. If she senses any fear in her stroker, her body will reactively respond as though there is cause for alarm.

How, then, do we maintain consciousness while increasing speed as a stroker? The same way we do everything in OM: we focus all of our attention on the point of connection between the clitoris and the finger. First, we drop our attention down to our pelvic floor, let our attention anchor there, then let it flow up through our body, out through the center of our stroking arm, and out of our finger. We create a circuit, grounded in our body so we don't "take off" along with the stroke. If we hold our primary attention anywhere other than our pelvic floor, our attention will be uprooted.

Next, we allow our attention to connect to the clitoris. We will feel a pull and allow our finger to move with it. If we are plugged into our own center and the connection, we will feel our finger lock on, seeming to beg to move of its own accord, as though we have an automatic twitch in our finger. We keep our focus here without hardening our attention. There may be all manner of expression coming from the strokee—trembling or tears or even screams. The key is to keep our focus on the point of connection. We do not want to leave her midway; if we do, she may lock up further. Instead, these bodily and vocal expressions are the call to increase the speed of the stroke.

There is a promise in OM: because tumescence will always try to preserve itself, provided we have an agreement with our partner to use speed, we can always debrief the OM afterward to hear what worked for each partner. Things often look different on the other side of the sound barrier. Eros will convert the tumescence. It's important to remember OM's promise. Although we will likely want to stop or slow down, to stop or slow down is detrimental here. Her system will lock that much more, and the momentum we have gained will now go into the lock.

21.
MEDIUM-SPEED STROKES

Medium-speed strokes have a restorative quality to them. They allow us to return to our homeostatic range, to integrate our experience, and to land. There is a feeling in a medium stroke of being entirely within our range. Feeling at home, we can afford to explore.

When we are first opening and exploring new spots, medium speed is often best. We can also practice agility in terms of the stroking directions we use, working in stages and using a medium-speed stroke. This provides an experience similar to connecting to the breath in meditation. Because this stroke is steady and familiar, it keeps the nervous system calm, smoothing it so we can anchor the mind and prevent ourselves from becoming overwhelmed.

Don't be fooled, however, into believing medium-speed strokes are only for beginners and will lead to a mediocre OM. A medium-speed, medium-pressure OM done with precision, care, and proper technique can open infinite doorways of sensation. In fact, it is in the medium range where we are able to best practice and increase our skill.

With medium-speed strokes, we pay attention to whether we are attempting to remain where we feel comfortable, avoiding growth. "Medium" is where this tendency is most prevalent so instead of remaining stuck in comfort, we can simply listen for what's being asked for at the point of contact.

22.
SLOW STROKES

Slow strokes are useful when a system is entirely free of tumescence. In this scenario, a slow OM is the ultimate tool to enter, deepen, and gain precision in the various spots. A slow stroke is a wonderful way to tune into the nuances and depths of a sensation. If the space inside the OM has been properly opened—meaning there has been lift-off from the tumescent barrier—what we find is that in a slow stroke, we can sink in. The deeper truths that are hidden in the body can rise up and reveal themselves in the space that is created in a slow stroke.

Emotions and longings can have the time and space to rise from the depths, becoming dynamic, alive chords that blend in with the sensations of the body. We are able to touch more subtle aspects of sensation in these slower tempos. While we use speed to enter a field of sensation, we use slowness to explore its texture, opening a conversation with it, letting it inform us in greater depth about the workings of its interior.

So it is in this slowness that our felt sense becomes informed. Our mind is brought to a sensation and shown that when we push forward or pull back, tighten or soften, penetrate or draw in, the sensation shifts. Through this feedback loop, we come to understand our inner workings as well as how to stroke and be stroked—not just at the physical level but within our interior world. We gain fluency in sensation that translates into being able to read the needs, hungers, and desires of the body.

In *detumesced* slowness—where the blockage to pure, direct, real-time feeling has been removed—we experience space outside the traffic jam of our thoughts. The mind has space to soften and to become supple again, rediscovering its permeability to life. If, however, the body is in a tumescent grip, slow strokes only work to make one more comfortable inside that grip—because there is no threat of breaking through the barrier to the unknown. There may be a sense of great relief, but the relief is the rational mind's relief that it got its way, got its speed, and is no longer threatened with Eros taking possession. The rational mind can now escape into the higher realms.

The addicted form of slow strokes is control. In this form, slow strokes become a demand, a means of controlling the flow of the OM. Those who are addicted to control can only maintain control at slow speeds and will employ drastic measures to ensure Eros isn't activated. They are in an uncomfortable state, like driving with feet on the brakes and the gas. They keep power down to a trickle the rational mind can manage.

Those who are addicted to control are unable to meet OM with their body; the body carries with it the mind's terror of being out of control. For them, the experience must all take place in the mind, where every move can be vigilantly watched. The rational mind cannot track anything above a slow speed. The grip of the mind has closed around the strokee and the stroker, rendering the stroker incapable of getting them out. It is a total lockdown.

If we received prior permission to break through tumescence using speed, now is the time. If we don't, and have instead agreed to have comfort OMs, we employ a slower speed. If there isn't an opening at this point, it's suggested we stop the OM. A person with a locked-down system, who continues to be stroked without conscious agreement, will experience being stroked as a violation despite having given consent and remaining in the nest.

If the strokee wants to continue, we can reset the container. It's essential to underline that the strokee must give express verbal permission to continue being stroked, because one of the symptoms of a locked-down system is a sense of powerlessness—as she is, in fact, without power. Her power is locked down. It is important to understand that when having a slow OM from a place of wanting control, we are never actually breaking into the Erotic zone where we can burn off tumescence. OM then becomes a system of pain management where nothing will improve; this is not the healing method of OM.

Once again we have a decision to make. If we do employ the speed that will activate Eros and convert tumescence, are we willing to take responsibility for our experience? Repeatedly confirming consent with our stroker is also key; doing so holds the greatest potential to unlock a gripped system. However, the price of admission is full responsibility for the discomfort the strokee will face in the process.

Once our system is open, we are free to explore all speeds. Our body will engage with us in the play of call-and-response where we sense a desired speed and adjust accordingly. We will be able to "play by ear" instead of by basic need or habit. The body will become infinitely more agile in response and slow strokes will be restored to their purpose of opening and deepening our relationship with sensation.

23.
MISUSING SPEED AND WHAT BECOMES AVAILABLE THROUGH SPEED USED WELL

It is radical to discover that, on the other side of the tumescent wall, few—if any—of the problems and fears that can lock up a strokee even exist. When we break through that wall, she will likely experience a freedom she has rarely known. We are asked to listen to the sensation but not to listen to her discomfort. We need to be incredibly sensitive—but within this sensitivity we must employ the method that will actually end the discomfort, not the method that will only make her more comfortable in her discomfort.

Speed in an OM shows us two things: how locked down a strokee's system is, and how much courage a stroker has. We also can see where speed is the result of fear and is the toxic mimic of actual speed. The way to tell if speed is being used well is to notice how open our solar plexus is. Are we breathing? How smooth is our stroke? There should be a flow to the employment of a fast stroke, an effortlessness we ride on. In fear-driven speed, there is a holding of the breath, a kinking of Erotic power coming from our center. As a result, there is no flow, and the power we need for the stroking finger is cut off.

If we tend to be speed-addicted, where the only way we can find activation is through speed, a simple remedy is to note the sensations we feel. Speed addiction is caused by a fear of fear coupled with a fear of sadness. The antidote to unconscious speed is sensing so we employ our mind in this way, letting it take off and break from the body's restrictions. We note heat, light, and vibration as well as texture and direction.

Also note whether the strokee enters climax with speed. This is not a sign of an open system, but rather of a locked-down system aiming to expel energy before it can reach the depths of tumescence. If this is the case, keep stroking at climax. It is important to communicate to the mind that it cannot introduce climax as a means of stopping action.

For a good period of time, we will likely be liberating speed from tumescence, either using it to break free of the tumescent barrier or to break free of the way speed compels us to race past sensation. Once speed is liberated, it becomes an unbelievable tool in terms of unconditionality and freedom. When the mind releases its brakes and has agility, it can move with the speed of a stroke until it becomes one with it. It's like a car traveling alongside a fast-moving train: when they are moving at the same speed, a sense of stillness occurs. It's also like riding a horse— the gallop has a hypnotic effect on the thinking brain, and then there is a sense of becoming one with motion.

The gift of speed in OM is that it moves faster than the rational mind. Speed can bring us into aspects of consciousness we could otherwise never access since we are typically subject to the rational mind's endless prohibitions. In the territory of the rational mind, we will never discover who we are or, more importantly, what we are made of.

Employing speed comes with a warning: we must not do it unless we are willing to genuinely take it on. Only we can guarantee we will not abandon ourselves. On one hand, for those interested in entering the Erotic body, speed is the only way to get where we are going. On the other hand, if we intend on quitting partway through or making excuses for why we need to slow down, speed will occur as a disruption in consciousness. There is a mind that wakes up in speed that can be woken up in no other way. If we are going to break through, we must continue to stroke with speed, with a consciousness employed to connect speed to the sensation that would prevent and absorb the energy of climax.

If we cannot affirm we will go until we break through, the suggestion is firm but honest: OM might not be the right practice and we ought not to do it. Only we can guarantee whether or not we will abandon ourselves. If we do choose to OM, we should likely do it as a means of making ourselves more comfortable in our tumescence, and thus should only stick to slow strokes where the rational mind will not be disturbed.

For the advanced practitioner, who is what we call *detumesced*, there is in fact no place safer than in speed, because there is no other way to activate the sixth-sense awareness in action. For this level of OM, incredible speed can feel like sinking into an ancient, slow, eternal knowing. Once this is awakened, there is nowhere we can go that is not pleasurable. Until we do, there is nowhere we can go that is pleasurable.

24.

PRESSURE:
ANCHORING THE MIND IN FEELING

Pressure is one of the most challenging and vital aspects we work with in OM. We speak of three pressures—heavy, medium, and light. Heavy pressure is still no firmer than how we would stroke an eyelid, whereas a light stroke has the delicateness with which we might touch an eyeball.

For the untrained attention, heavy pressure is the default, initial pressure used. Much of the world operates on heavy pressure, so our attention cannot initially perceive lighter pressure. One exception is when the person has tumescent trauma, which causes the senses to be overly sensitized rather than desensitized. Even the lightest pressure is uncomfortable. In that case, the sense gates have "locked open" instead of being able to open and shut. The exposed nervous system then must remain in constant contact with the environment; consequently, it becomes raw from overstimulation.

People in this overly sensitized state over-hear sounds and so the slightest sound sets them on edge. They over-feel sensations so that virtually any sensation occurs as an irritant. And, in this overly sensitized state, they also over-expose visuals. Without the capacity to open and close the sense gates with ease, they lack the capacity both to stop the steady stream of stimuli—and the resulting activation of the nervous system—and are unable to process what they have perceived. Instead, stimuli continue to build and build, making the nervous system more rigid.

What "hurts" in this case is actually the nervous system's rigidity. The pain is the result of the incoming stimuli hitting up against an impermeable and impacted system that has been locked open and is unable to stop the stream. People open in this way live in a permanent state of rigid hyperarousal. The normal intake and release of stimuli through a permeable membrane of perception is hindered, and they feel like they are living in a state of slight electrical shock. Given our cultural predisposition against *down*—taking time and space to allow oneself to step out of the onslaught of life and let go of control—and the few acceptable means of accessing the down, most women are stuck in a state that has altered the body's normal and healthy relationship with heavy pressure.

Two exaggerated responses may occur. The first occurs in those who only respond to heavy pressure, whose sense gates are so impacted with undigested material that they cannot otherwise respond. The energetic request issuing from these individuals is for increased pressure and speed. The underlying aim of their request is to activate the hyperdrive of the climax impulse in order to bypass their rigidity so that a massive discharge can occur in one "dump." Their system is so rigid or inflexible that the dynamism necessary to sense nuanced sensation is all but impossible. It doesn't register.

For these nervous systems, we do in fact employ heavy pressure, but at a consistently slow or medium speed so as to *milk out* the excess material rather than *blow it out* in a climax. The reason we do this is because the activation of the impulse of habituated climax often overrides the mind's capacity to track sensation. It is virtually impossible for the untrained mind to track real-time sensation at the level of sensation that occurs after activation. The mind is unyoked from the harness of the body and races over the present stroke to get to its perceived goal. The aim of medium speed, then, is to remain under the radar of climax activation so the sense gates can relax and material can be released, but the mind can still track the stroke.

One thing for the stroker to keep in mind is that heavy pressure and increased speed may produce more dramatic expression, sound, or trembling from the strokee. This can be mesmerizing for an appearance-based stroker who doesn't yet know how to sense deeper sensation and instead relies on what can be observed on the surface. In OM, we are not going for greater drama, but for greater depth of sensation, which will provide for greater connection, intimacy, and entry into the Erotic mind.

We don't want to become stuck at the physical level; while it may appease the "quick fix" tumescent mind, which wants the fast reward of seeing an impact, this appeasement is fleeting and will never be gratifying in the long run. We will get a "hit" but that hit comes at a price; a hard come-up brings a hard come-down. Once we become habituated to heavy pressure on the physical level, we have to continue increasing pressure in order to provoke sensation, with diminishing results. We also become a slave to appearances, robbing ourselves of the opportunity to learn to feel into the feeling states of other human beings. We will be doing the equivalent of playing air guitar when we could instead become a master musician.

In order to fit into what titillates her stroker, the strokee learns to perform sensation—not as a means of activation, but as a means of concealing that she cannot feel. The conditioning of the tumescent mind in a woman locks in with the conditioning of the stroker's tumescent mind. Those who are prisoners of the world of appearances have overly used the perceptual gate of vision while the other gates remain closed, robbing the body of all its resources that would otherwise be distributed evenly throughout and activate the sixth center of the Erotic sense. The sixth sense is an antenna of intimacy and involves intuitive or connected awareness.

It is an either-or equation: if the senses are hijacked by visual displays, the exchange in an OM will be a visual performance of sensation that isn't actually felt, performed for someone who in turn cannot sense there is no actual feeling beneath the performance. The feedback loop then remains at this surface level, never descending to the level of intimacy where two human beings feel each other.

The climax impulse in the untrained mind thus has a great potential for habituation. It is not that it makes us habituated; rather, it's more that the flood of sensation is so strong the untrained mind gets washed away. We are left with an unconscious reflex for losing control that we are now reliant on as our only means of letting go.

In contrast, a mind anchored in the capacity to truly feel all speeds, pressures, and spots has other means of release and delight. Rather than needing to escape the present stroke, it grows to be strong and steady enough to withstand, and stay conscious for, climax.

The second exaggerated response comes from a strokee who is overstimulated to the point that she is locked in hyperarousal and asks for only light pressure. She may not even be able to take direct contact. The unintuitive stroke for her is steady, heavy pressure—to crack through the hardened layer of tumescence, and even more importantly, to allow the locked-open sense gates to close. The strokee may be sure, even demanding, that she can only take light pressure. This does absolutely nothing other than stroke the tumescence itself. As with speed, gaining permission and ascertaining whether our partner's intention is to enter the Erotic body or to have her tumescence stroked, is highly advisable. Setting a safe word is also wise.

Should we proceed, know that when there is the demand for this type of light pressure, the tumescence itself is talking. It works to allow for greater disassociation: there is just enough contact to fulfill the body's need for contact, but not enough to activate the Erotic body. The charge then activates and ensures the tumescent mind's need for control, giving it more fuel. At that point, the tumescent mind may then go off into fantasy or ideas of bliss that are in fact entirely disconnected from the body.

A woman in this condition requires regular, medium-to-heavy pressure strokes of medium speed to begin to enter the body she has been locked out of. There will likely be expressions of parasympathetic activation—from shaking to flushing and contractions—because a woman who is locked in hyperarousal has a locked introitus. Therefore, the normal fluttering that would happen with each stroke doesn't occur. She is either locked open or locked gripping down. We are instead aiming for fluttering waves throughout the OM that match the intensity of stroke and speed. This matching reaction is incontrovertible feedback that the strokee's mind is connected to the body and that the body is driving.

Until we reach this fluidity, we cannot start an actual OM—we are instead in the period of "playing scales." It may take years to open the response. Anything we do beyond scales will be of little use, although it may add visual stimulation. However, sensation cannot be truly perceived until the body is open; it will just add more undigested material into an already overly taxed system. It's important to take the time to build the foundation on an open system.

25.
HEAVY PRESSURE

We experience heavy pressure in three primary ways: our body going into overdrive, our mind disconnecting from our body, or we may experience an energy of punishment. When applied with a lack of strength and steadiness, heavy pressure results in more damage than good. Heavy pressure is quite challenging to apply well, however, using it well, like a good surgical technique, can be beneficial.

We can use heavy pressure as a surgical skill in OM; a skilled "surgeon" must be able to cut through the skin, so to speak, without harming the organs inside. There is a power and finesse to the activity, but the main activity is the capacity to increase rather than decrease the senses. Frequently, when we use heavy pressure, we wind up decreasing the sensation. As the stroker, we do not want our finger to drag, rub, or press; we want steadiness throughout, requiring a firm stroking, not rubbing motion, that is consistent from the top to the bottom of the clitoris, with a smoothness as we come back down to the bottom. This motion builds steady waves throughout the body. The waves then activate the stuck tumescent energy, rendering it dynamic where it was previously locked.

The key to heavy pressure is to understand we are using it for two reasons. One, we wish to cut through the strokee's thick layer of tumescence to get to a level where most of the tumescence in her body has been converted to be dynamic rather than stuck. Two, we aim to provide a ballast to go into the "down" spots. Heavy pressure paired with a slower stroke, for instance on the nine o'clock or six o'clock spots, can bring about the depths of an OM as opposed to the heights.

It is crucial not to add anything extra, while remaining incredibly aware of the tendency to do so. There is a fine line between giving the strokee heavy pressure that penetrates the tumescence holding her hostage, and the kind of aggression that is ignoring her response and seeks only to know its own impact.

Interestingly, while each requires a type of depersonalization, one aims to, in an impersonal way, cut through tumescence to get to the tender nervous system locked behind it, while the other neglects the nervous system's response. The issue is: there are so few individuals well-trained in heavy pressure that women may feel disregarded by their partners or find themselves locked in tumescence. And if we then conflate the tumescence with the woman, the tumescence begins to erode the confidence of the stroker. The stroker in turn ends up frustrated or angry with the strokee, and the real culprit of tumescence is never caught. We can neither cater to and stroke too lightly nor become angry and add punishment to the pressure.

We also cannot go unconscious in the face of tumescent discomfort, disconnecting and dragging the finger. This pressure is due to a lack of consciousness, not because consciousness is guiding with firmness.

26.
MEDIUM PRESSURE

Medium pressure is used for several purposes, including to find a basic connection between partners, to find a spot to integrate a high or low peak, or to ground and comfort in a general way. Medium pressure is the equivalent to a bath that is body temperature. The aim is to have the finger feel so fluid and buttery that it melts into the spot and there is a simple, calming connection.

The bread-and-butter stroke—the stroke we return to in order to integrate—uses medium pressure and medium speed. Each strokee has a slightly different internal setting for what medium is, but for the most part it's a slight indentation in the skin that registers as a tiny amount of friction—just enough to stir up an electromagnetic sensation.

Don't be afraid to go to medium pressure at any point. Many strokers have a tendency to want to get fancy with big, looping ups and crescendos down, but it's possible to have an OM life entirely composed of medium pressure and experience the opening and connection to the Erotic mind. That opening and connection is the only purpose. The Erotic mind will take us where it and we want to go, while fanciful strokes are often an impediment.

There is nothing that is more exalted, spectacular, or awe-inspiring than being present in the moment with this stroke, right now. It doesn't matter whether we bang on the door to the Erotic mind or gently tap it; all that matters is that it opens. The glory is found in what happens when the door opens, and when it opens, our finger will be guided beyond what we could ever have consciously thought to do. On this side of the door, the key is to do whatever we do well, diligently guided by sensation and avoiding adding anything extra.

What makes us feel good about ourselves on this side proves to be empty on the other side. We must not fall into the trap of thinking we can perform the inexpressible joy and freedom that happens in the Erotic mind when it moves our hand for us: the mind is elevated to see things it has never seen, through a body that feels things it has never felt. The mind requires more work on the front end to find the skill, precision, and interest in the simple, medium-pressure stroke—to find an entire world in what could seem boring or repetitive, coming back to refresh our attention every time. This, though, is how we turn the mundane into the magical. We have no need to create spectacular conditions; instead, we train the mind to find the obedience it needs to see the spectacular in the mundane.

With medium-pressure strokes, we need to pay attention to whether we are being overly cautious and using them to avoid venturing into other pressures or using them to maintain a sense of comfort rather than to create growth. And with medium speed, we can be lulled into a complacency where we aren't growing because we aren't feeling the fear of the unknown.

In those scenarios, we may become stuck in this pocket and, invariably, we receive diminishing returns. Soon, we are only stroking for superficial or physical pleasure, and the element of Eros that gives OM dimension and complexity is lost. When this happens we are no longer OMing—we are merely stroking genitals. The antidote is to return to listening, at the point of contact, to what is being asked for. It's quite simple because it's always changing. It can take a moment to recognize the only thing that brings gratification is growth, but the moment we tap back into the point of contact, we remember.

27.
LIGHT PRESSURE

A light-pressure stroke can only be truly perceived by a mind that has been emptied and has been placed in a body where the senses permeate so that the body is an open state of potential, like a pond. It requires great power to stroke lightly and steadily. With too little power, the stroke will be shaky or will hover, tickling rather than connecting.

The purpose of light pressure with speed is to gain liftoff, as if the sensation has wings. From here the sensation begins to open and spread outward. Light pressure is associated with expansion, whereas heavy pressure is associated with density.

We may apply light pressure with an ultraslow or even nonmoving stroke, allowing the stroke to take us into stillness and silence. Light pressure showcases and evokes more of what is already present.

Using light pressure, it can be challenging for many to find the sweet spot where connection remains yet the stroke doesn't become "squeaky," meaning the stroke lacks fluidity. In that case, too much self-consciousness goes to the finger. Rather than having a soft, gliding quality, the finger locks on the top or the bottom of the stroke and sensation collects in it so it grows heavier. Here, we can simply do a longer light stroke at this point to move the energy that has collected.

The key with a light stroke is to connect to the stillness inside our partner, which pulls out the softness in our finger. We connect by imagining our finger can open and can allow what's deep inside of us to be pulled forth. Once we do that, we will sense a lock-on connection, which can then be extracted through our stroking finger.

It can be easy to confuse a light stroke with bliss, so it's crucial to note whether we are feeling a light stroke in our head or in our body. The sensation may collect in the head, where we get the feeling of being "high"; this feeling is not actually a high but rather a signal that we aren't connected to the body. When we do a light stroke correctly, the entire body will feel, on the one hand, as if it is weighted down, and on the other, as if it is lifting off. We are not a helium balloon flying away. We are more like a flower opening to the sun.

28.
GIVING GOOD HEAVY PRESSURE IS AN ART

Because we have a prejudice against down, we tend not to honor the fact that our bodies and minds need to come down, and that a primary route is through deliberate, conscious, heavy pressure. We observe this in life, where if we do not consciously find time to let go and release the corset of our ideas about who we are and who we should be, we will unconsciously create experiences that will apply the heavy pressure needed for us to release them. We may get ill from overwork, or fired from a job we checked out on instead of quitting when we knew we wanted to. But instead of facing the discomfort of loss or change, we grip to what we know. Our fear of heavy pressure makes us unable to penetrate tumescence or delusion; we have thus become a world of hypersensitive people, demanding only the lightest touch.

As a result, our bodies and minds lack resilience. We experience a preciousness that demands more preciousness. There comes to be an extremist's version not only of the care required to not upset tumescence, but also of legislating against any natural form of the expression of pressure. The result: we are taken hostage by tumescence, experiencing everything from oversensitivity to over-emotionality and hysteria as we remove access to Eros, our only defense against tumescence.

When tumescence rules the roost without the option of heavy pressure, our consciousness grows brittle and legalistic. We accept fewer and fewer outlets for spontaneous expression. We don't develop the resilience that could absorb and even enjoy any behavior. We fail to realize we have become merely a host doing the bidding of tumescence, which demands control. A natural connection that would dissolve tumescence is all but impossible.

Tumescence creates teacup people who shatter easily. The pressure of control is so great that everything hurts. The concept of deliberate, heavy pressure—which would relax constricted nerve endings—is nonexistent. Instead, the idea of pressure is conflated with that of threat or violation.

Because we dismiss the need to come down, we don't consciously learn how to do the stroke that will bring us down. Heavy pressure then either becomes unconscious—a pressure that is hard and fast and lacking attention—or it is delivered with a meanness—a pressure with a punitive quality to counteract the irritation of being on the receiving end of oversensitivity. In this case, rather than decreasing tumescence, heavy pressure compounds it.

Applying heavy pressure well is an art few know. It requires, first and foremost, a strength and steadiness of attention that is rooted in a fundamental "rightness": we know the strokee is locked inside a cage with a bear wrapped around her, and we want to get the bear off without harming our friend. We cannot let an ounce of fear in, as our friend might think we're after them and add to the difficulty. We want to stun the tumescence because what it lives on is the fear of its host.

In the places where we are likely to add unconscious pressure, even more attention is required. We want to apply a steady attention as if we are wielding a sword; we want a swiftness in the cut and we need to be aware of where we are aiming. We want to remember we are doing this as a means of cutting away the tumescence that surrounds our friend in order to free her for greater connection.

It's important to depersonalize the tumescence, remembering it has our friend in its clutches and that it—tumescence—is the offending quality, not our friend. With deliberate, focused, firm attention, tumescence can be converted and made into an ally.

Effective heavy pressure is never given to hurt our friend, to make a point, or to feel our own impact. It is given because it is what is being called for in direct proportion to the level of tumescence that has built up, and it will either destroy connection or be a force that builds it.

Many strokees ask for lighter pressure. Or they ask for heavy pressure—but only to climax. What their bodies often want is a steady, deeply conscious pressure that is without an agenda and without anger. Like in a massage, this kind of pressure opens the muscles and relaxes the mind.

If a strokee trembles or shakes in an OM, it's the result of tumescence releasing from the musculature. Don't be frightened; this is good. If the trembling and shaking becomes writhing and performance, lighten the pressure. Heavy pressure must be goalless. The feeling of cutting through tumescence is like a great exhale. We will notice a clarity of mind and of sensation. An OM does not truly begin until tumescence is breached, because otherwise we are only stroking the tumescence. In that case, nothing actually reaches our essence, where contact ignites Eros.

29.
DOWNSTROKES

Because we have a predisposition against down, it's easy to mistake a downstroke as a punishment. At the height of sensation, the instruction to stroke down seems counterintuitive: at the crescendo, the moment where the relief of the wave crashing down would feel like the reward with its cascade of endorphins, we instead reverse the direction of the stroke and drop down a few notches. Or, if our partner is in a state of anticipation, brimming with electricity and excitement, we may start with a downstroke. Rather than shaking with excitement, the electricity is brought down where it is steadied and held in the solidity of the body. For the tumescent mind, there is a formula: to experience excitement, keep building it until there is an explosion and a relief. To then stroke down instead suggests to the tumescent mind that it has lost its only potential for relief.

Eros operates on another model. It stays with and grows our range of enjoyment, prior to the anxiety of excitement, so we are no longer living in a state that seeks relief. This model happens when we are brought down into the bones and sinew of the body, where there is comfort and safety. As we come to know this well, it's no longer a state we are trying to escape; instead, it's a state we rest inside of.

Downstrokes bring us down into the world of feelings and unexamined experiences. Because the body never lies, we are brought face-to-face with our emotions, and to the wisdom our emotions were aiming to draw us into. We discover the fear we previously tried to escape was what was drawing us to the deepest level of resilience, and the lust we couldn't outrun was actually the source from which all attraction issues.

Downstrokes bring us to the emotional reactivity, even outrage, that wants to draw us down into the power to be with injustice in such a way we can heal it rather than perpetuate it. Downstrokes bring us down into the truths we know could set us free, where we will either flail or fall into the arms of Eros, depending on our relationship to the below. Those who have discovered that this is where we find the bedrock of truth—the landing pad of the body where we relax, refresh, and integrate—meet the downstroke as we would a lover whose arms we might fall into. The downstroke is where we can finally let go and abandon the effort. The downstroke signifies we will be home soon.

In the exalted form, downstrokes are associated with surrender, which is the engaged act of offering ourselves to experience exactly as it is. There is a sense of being at the mercy of something, in the same way we are at the mercy of gravity, with a force pulling us down that speeds up the descent more than if we were on flat ground. This surrender can be alternately terrifying and thrilling. That quality of conquering and climbing that is part of an upstroke is swallowed into this downward motion. When we lie down for an OM, after our daily life that can leave us buzzing above our bodies and outside of our minds, the first downstroke collects us back into the warm bath of the body, where we can concurrently let go and collect ourselves.

We spend so much of our lives believing detachment and dissociation are as good as it gets, and we keep pumping for joy until we have only fumes left to run on. It finally gets so uncomfortable that we must altogether detach. But a good downstroke can take that frantic, manic mind, which trembles and shakes and runs when we try to connect to it, and bring it into the safe warmth of the body. The anxiousness we might call ecstasy or bliss is replaced with a deep and abiding comfort. With the feeling of contact between finger and clitoris, both partners get to exhale as they drop down a few flights and are able to simply be.

30.
UNDERSTANDING DOWNSTROKES THROUGH OM

A downstroke is, literally, a stroke in the downward direction, toward earth and the introitus.

Knowing how to go down well is a vital skill in Eros. Going down well means going down deliberately. After having been in an expanded state, we are going to come down one way or another, so when we do it deliberately, we remove the panic of descent. When attention is added, the storms located in the body—anger, power, arousal, Eros—that we normally avoid, convert into measures of the Erotic state that include power, strength, stability, and intensity.

Through our attention, these storms become harnessed, just as a knowledgeable sailor harnesses wind. The storms move us where we wish to go: deeper and deeper into the Erotic state of consciousness, which is steeped in eternal and interdependent connection. Through making our way down, we find ourselves at the location of power—where desire and fear issue from. We are in the primal form of ourselves. This is the position from which love issues, as do turn-on and human connection. The bottom is where we get fueled.

Moving down is an act of falling or being carried, and it must be initiated by something outside of ourselves. Just as we cannot tickle or massage ourselves, so too, we cannot bring ourselves out of control. To force ourselves down is not falling but rather lying down: it can be restful, but ultimately, it is an act of fear. This is not to say there isn't an art to falling, which is why the dancer, athlete, and martial artist recognize the great grace in falling. The key, though, is to have an intimacy with the motion of going down. We create this intimacy by taking each stroke to the point of completion. We often jump off before reaching the top or the bottom. We have an idea of what it will feel like and we mentally leap ahead, leaving the stroke altogether.

This giving up early is the result of not building trust with each stroke, and it plays out in all of life. The full stroke can feel too vulnerable. Maybe we sense we don't have as much power as we hoped, or that we could have more. When we stay beyond the point we would normally hop off, power is the self-discovery that happens. Our trust—or lack thereof—in the downstroke reveals our relationship with power. We either do the equivalent of holding our breath, not letting the stroke take us to the place where we fall apart, or we let the downstroke take us; we come apart and are then rebuilt in the upstroke. As the stroker, we address this by making the downstroke a little longer than the upstroke, holding attention more on the downstroke.

If we physically over-stroke on the downstroke, we bottom out with a feeling of heaviness or dullness. The dynamic sense of tension is absent. The instruction here is to tease the energy, meaning we connect to the spot and progressively draw it out, becoming lighter again. We match exhales for stabilization and stroke down with a feeling of deep, dark, rich earthiness.

31.
UPSTROKES

When rooted in the body, upstrokes occur as transcendence. They offer a sensory peak from the summit of what is possible without being constrained by gravity. We sense the world at the level of potential, which gives us motivation to shed extra or stagnant energy. We have a sense of the wind at our back, as if we have hydraulics and are being lifted when we would habitually climb or push. We are lifted by the Erotic state beyond where we could bring ourselves.

Here, we are more energy than physicality, while still being deeply rooted in the body. This rootedness confers a feeling of safety that rounds out the feeling of freedom that might otherwise erode into anxiety. Anxiety is the place where we want to stay up, up, up, but it becomes jittery. When rooted in this way, the sensation itself is full-bodied and not just a single note. The edge is taken off. In life, we are often trained in only one direction: up. We think the solution to the issues caused by having gone too far up is to go farther up. We feel anxious or that there is something in the depths calling for our attention. We feel a tension or even a mania. Sometimes, we even call this bliss or euphoria.

The freedom associated with up is not in any way high, dizzy, or spacey; it is clarity. Up starts with a feeling of love, richness, or reverence that we are, tiny stroke by stroke, extending. The truth is, the mind can only assimilate the smallest stroke. This is how we expand our capacity—in the same way we expand our lung capacity by increasing the flexibility of the cavity by drawing in the breath fully and exhaling fully, not by inhaling and holding our breath. We do this with each stroke, feeling one stroke at a time.

The capacity for this kind of liftoff, this kind of lightness, is key to offering the inspiration of Eros. Without this liftoff, our OMs have a deadly earnestness and gravity—or a fixed quality that adheres to the physical, whereas the sensation we seek is found only in the activation of the Erotic body.

Up is where we can "see" the wisdom from below. We may have moments of insight or intuition with the upstroke, including how to best meet the stroke. Down is where the circuit breaker is, and up is where the lights go on.

As the upstroke starts, it can feel especially subtle and require deeper attention. An upstroke has the quality of magnetizing the clitoris to the finger, pulling energy up to the surface and out through the body. There is an overall feeling of liftoff, elevation, and then breaking through the clouds of the tumescent mind. The sense is spacious, quiet, and open.

An important instruction is to move the attention along with the stroke rather than moving our attention ahead of it and attempting to pull the stroke to a conclusion. When this grip happens, the antidote is to lift the stroking finger for a second and allow a moment of descent and relaxation. We can then take in the breath and sensation with tiny sips. The instruction to lift asks us to raise the finger just barely off the clitoris to where only a tiny synapse of the lubricant exists between them. Notice how the current still flows through the lubricant neutrally without physical touch.

On the downstroke, we allow ourselves to be moved again. We can become so nestled into the down that our attention goes lax and, as a result, we don't show up for the upstroke when it comes. We end up feeling hunkered down or almost like we are drowning. We feel powerless, without realizing we are in fact drowning in power, and that the way to feel relief is to use the power to go back up and see what we gathered in the down.

A good upstroke is extraordinarily crisp in sending and receiving. It is tight and deliberate. It has a strength without rigidity and does not allow itself to be carried by the unconscious program, which only wants to go up and over. We discover the more we can go up without going over, the more spacious and steady the upstroke becomes, and the more reality reveals itself to us.

32.
THE FELT EXPERIENCE OF PRESSURES, SPEEDS, AND DIRECTIONS

Each pressure, speed, and direction has a unique felt sensation in the body. Whether it's the grounding nature of heavy pressure, the clarity of medium speed, or the release of a downstroke, each aspect offers a unique pathway to a deeper understanding of the experience inside the body, where we are attuned, overly attuned, or not attuned.

Heavy Pressure

Heavy pressure feels like earth, bone, emotion, the mysterious. It is concentrated. If we are not attuned to it, we may lack passion, have a challenging time showing up during difficulties, be a person who seeks spiritual bypasses, be disembodied in either the intellectual or spiritual realm, and have difficulties with the feminine and with control. If we are overly attuned, we may be overly emotional, feel a lot of heavy internal pressure and/or shame, feel we are at the mercy of life, and believe we need the weight of the world pressing down upon us to compel us to respond.

Medium Pressure

Medium pressure is clear, indicates digestion, feels integrated, and is grounded. If we are not attuned, we may feel dissipated or dysregulated, have either ideals or emotions we are unable to bring to the surface, and experience scattered attention or a feeling of impotence.

Light Pressure

Light pressure has a feeling of reverence, dreams, ideas, and the illumined, and is diffuse. If we are not attuned, we may lack intuition, be unable to sense subtle realms, and feel stuck on earth. If we are overly attuned, we may be hypersensitive, fussy, easily irritated, require special circumstances in order for us to let go, feel pride, and have a need to reject the world.

Slow Speed

Slow speed feels akin to depth and likes to get inside of things. If we are not attuned, we tend to live on the surface, are moved by appearances, and may feel hyper or impulsive. If we are overly attuned, we may be controlling, demanding, prone to anger, need to withdraw regularly, and be addicted to depth in relationships.

Medium Speed

Medium speed feels as though we are embodied and has the marks of integration. If we are not attuned, we may be flighty, as if we are unable to land, and, though we are ready to try everything, we are unable to generate real traction. If we are overly attuned, we are stuck in the horizontal, need more variety in the material realm in order to stay interested, and are overly focused on the mundane.

Fast Speed

Fast speed feels like height together with motion or flow. If we are not attuned, we may feel put upon when things move quickly, scared and anxious and wanting to stop the action, and confused when there is movement—hiding our confusion behind irritation and feeling rejected.

If we are overly attuned, we are likely to be manic, anxious, and unnecessarily driven, rolling over people and experiences, and refusing to come down.

Up Direction

Upstrokes feel like taking in, building, inhaling, and holding on. If we are not attuned, we may need a lot of upstrokes if we are to respond and we may lack the levity to experience ease and the sublime. If we are overly attuned, we can only consume and may feel internally tight and stressed.

Down Direction

Downstrokes feel like release, falling apart, and letting go. If we are not attuned, we have a hard time letting go. We keep driving for things, experience indigestion, and have challenges with the feminine aspects of embodiment as well as with relaxation and non-production. If we are overly attuned, we are always falling apart, prone to sadness, and subject to sloth.

33.
UNDERSTANDING LENGTH

Strokes can range in length from zero millimeters to ten millimeters. Shorter strokes produce more sensation as there is more precise contact with the clitoris. Some of the more potent strokes are not even strokes at all; they are a placement of the finger at the spot where the pulsing of the body does the stroking, with no movement of the fingertip.

34.

THE STROKES

In OM, there are a myriad of strokes, each with its unique sensation and purpose. Through the exploration and combination of various speeds, pressures, directions, lengths, and locations, we learn to evoke and navigate the vast landscape of sensations that OM can offer. Each stroke, from the priming to the gravity, is a key that unlocks a different door into the realm of Eros, allowing us to experience the full spectrum of our Erotic selves. Together, these strokes help us cultivate a dynamic, intimate connection with the body, enabling us to engage in life.

Priming

Using the pad of the finger, we do the priming stroke, the starting stroke of the OM. We stroke down with long, broad, medium-speed, and medium-pressure downstrokes, focusing on the upper-left-hand quadrant of the clitoris. The sensation feels like scratching an itch and like sinking in. When we finish, there is a richness and a sense of completion.

Finding the Spot

Stroking in a meandering way, with a short, slow, and medium-pressure upstroke using the tip of our finger, gradually moving toward the one o'clock position, we find the spot. When we land there, we feel a jolt or a tingle beginning to radiate from under the skin as connection is made.

Butterfly

We use short, fast, and light upstrokes on the spot around the one o'clock position with the tip of the finger when doing the butterfly stroke. This stroke feels energizing, like carbonation or buzzing.

Home

Using the tip of the finger, we stroke with medium speed, medium pressure, medium-length upstrokes on the spot around the one o'clock position. This stroke feels comforting, like building energy, and has an "at home" feeling of rightness.

Reaching

Stroking with long, light, medium-speed upstrokes along the left side of the clitoris, from the six o'clock to twelve o'clock position, using the tip of the finger, we do the reaching stroke. This stroke feels like a "zing" with a rising off the floor, and it draws out a yearning and desire to come toward the finger.

Lower

Here, we stroke with long, light, medium-speed downstrokes in the vestibule underneath the clitoris using the tip of the finger. We experience a feeling of deep release and relief, as if we have been holding on to something and can now let go.

Deep

To do the deep stroke, we hold the tip of our finger still on the spot around the one o'clock position, using the precise amount of pressure called for. We experience a feeling of darkness and a smooth current of power, with waves of electricity and a sense of heavy relaxation.

Expansion

We stroke with very short, light, and medium-speed upstrokes, using the tip of the finger, on the spot around the one o'clock position. This expansion stroke feels breathless, like an opening, as if our cells are made of light, revving things up.

Stair

With the tip of the finger, we use fast and medium-speed, light, teasing-pressure upstrokes on the spot around the one o'clock position. The stair stroke feels like climbing, and we savor the growing hunger and anticipation we experience.

Summit

Here, we hold the tip of the finger with a light, teasing pressure around the one o'clock position. This feels like intense pleasure, as if we are nailed to the floor not wanting to move, with heat inside the body.

Love

We use the fingertip and pad of the finger, creating slow-to-medium speed, slightly more than medium pressure, medium-length downstrokes at the three o'clock position. There is a silky, fluid, warm, thick-like-honey feeling to the love stroke that is soothing and cozy.

Animation

Here, we stroke with medium to heavy pressure, medium length, slightly faster than medium-speed downstrokes at the very edge of the clitoris around the four to five o'clock position. These animation strokes feel earthy, human, delicious—like the energy of play.

Gravity

In a gravity stroke, we use long, slow, and heavy downstrokes broadly across the clitoris with the pad of the index finger. These strokes feel like a slow descent, like an elevator gently coming back to earth.

FOLLOWING THE SENSATION

35.
TURNING ON THE SPOT

When we enter the Erotic body, we touch a state of optionality and see, from a different vantage point, the inevitable simultaneity of repulsion and attraction. The issue isn't that these two qualities exist simultaneously, for this dynamic tension is what we call life. Instead, now we have allowed consciousness to be immersed in the spacious container of the body, which can concurrently hold and expand to include both qualities—repulsion and attraction—rather than regard them as polarized.

It all depends on whether or not the tools are in the hands of the tumescent mind, which operates with the mantra "separate and oppose" and positions the two forces of repulsion and attraction against each other, offering attention to only one at a time. In contrast, the Erotic mind aims to expand and include. But the tumescent mind sets up a tug-of-war between repulsion and attraction, where their natural, dynamic tension becomes tension—and tension alone. A kind of fixity emerges that locks the ability of either of these forces, repulsion or attraction, to effectively move us. We are confined to a cell, using these two forces as weapons of defense for the likes and dislikes that make up our identity in a paralyzing state of seeming contradiction.

When, on the other hand, these forces are in the hands of the Erotic mind, they operate for an altogether different purpose, moving us through the world not according to our preferences, but beyond them, into the complete maturation of being. The aim is to draw the two seemingly opposing forces into the concept of self as a means of knowing the self in unification, including knowing our own uniqueness. It is when we are pulled down into the Erotic realm, outside of the watchful eye of the "command and control" center of the tumescent mind—which uses attraction and repulsion to maintain a locked sense of self—that we have the potential to go beyond our most cherished convictions. This potential to go beyond, when pulled down into the Erotic realm, incites an internal revolution that evolves beyond the "old guard" dictatorship. This force takes us beyond our own resistance and into the heart of our humanity, where we reclaim what we have deemed unacceptable in ourselves as well as what we have been unwilling to own and love.

Reassigned from protecting a small identity, this force now appropriates attraction and repulsion, guiding the lower realms toward or away from anything depending on how it aligns with the Erotic self. These tendencies are in no way bad, but have been used by an unconscious and unskillful driver.

In OM, with the Erotic self as driver, we begin to practice the skill of pendulation. This involves weaving together seemingly opposing states. Rather than trying to maintain a pristine state alongside a profane state, we expand our reception to include both states. OM tells us that all we seek is here, right now in this very stroke, and the only thing missing is the capacity to receive it. Pendulation relieves us of the internal conflict that arises when we abandon one aspect of ourselves in favor of another.

The way we do this kind of pendulation is simple. We locate our home spot, the spot we often gravitate toward, because it's where we feel solid and secure. It may be the one o'clock spot, or at a more advanced level we may have found our own unique spot. We then locate a spot that repulses us. It may have a more pleasurable quality, which we see ourselves as too "spiritual" for. It may have the "in love" quality, which we turn away from because we often get stuck there. It may be a spot that is too subtle and that we find irritating. If a spot has been switched off, it can even appear "dead."

We stroke the home spot until it is well lit with a kind of valence around the spot that radiates outward. Next we move to the repulsion spot, almost as if we are dragging Eros from one spot to the other. We refer to this as "turning on the spot." Pendulation teaches us to recognize that every spot is uniquely beautiful, with each spot offering something vital to the whole.

If the whole is not lit up, we rely overly on the spots that are lit up. If our twelve o'clock spot is turned on but our six o'clock spot is not, we will have liftoff even when we need gravity. The twelve o'clock spot will become overtaxed and our response will not be on the spot of what wants to happen.

In order to light up the whole clitoris, we pendulate until the two spots are connected. It is as if we are hooking into a power source to bring electricity to another spot, until this other spot is itself switched on and capable of self-generating power. We do this until all the spots on the clitoris are connected and lit up. At this point there is a phase transition and the whole clitoris switches on. The clitoris becomes a source that pumps Eros into the body, until the sensation spreads to the whole of the body.

From here, we pendulate in terms of our speed. We may have a preference for a rapid speed and tend to check out when the stroking is slow. In that case, we alternate between fast and slow strokes until the ignition from one transfers to the other. We then move to pressure, going through and igniting all three pressures (heavy, medium, and light) on all spots. Finally, we include directions (upstrokes and downstrokes) until every spot is equally ignited at all speeds, all pressures, and in both directions. We have now liberated the clitoris and, by extension, the body. Instead of having the ability to merely move, the body now has the option to be moved according to the commands of the fully immersed Erotic self.

Then the consciousness beyond consciousness we call genius is able to move us into the deeper truth of the calling on each of us, without impediment. This is where we have the courage to not be defined by an identity rooted in culture, but to define a culture that goes beyond our separate identity, all while protecting the sanctity of our unique expression.

Just as each spot on the clitoris has a unique offering that is of the most benefit only when the whole is lit up, so too is our expression in this life.

36.
UNCONDITIONALITY

OM is a mind-training practice that teaches us to attune to life with equal, simultaneous attention at the level of sensation so that, through resonance, we can experience intimacy in each moment. We can live in pitch-perfect response. In OM, there are three speeds, three pressures, two directions, five lengths, and ten spots that in various combinations compose the sensory palate that plays throughout OM and our everyday lives.

Whatever we are able to maintain continuous connection with, we have facility with, and with facility comes a sense of freedom. Where our attention is unable to properly track and connect, we experience reactivity in the form of grasping, rejection, and checking out; we feel at the mercy of our ingrained responses, rather than feeling we have a choice.

The intention of OM, then, is to develop an attention that can accurately track and remain with sensation continuously in the face of not only a reality that changes, but one that changes in relationship. In OM, the attention is being trained in the high art of moving with all gradients of sensation while participating as its conduit in a mutually influencing relationship. This is a key aspect of OM because it sets new grooves in the mind that prime it for relationships based in interdependency between two poles. The mind is used to collapsing into the extremes—the default states of stifling union or demagnetized separation that cannot substitute for genuine, dynamic tension. Developing this kind of attention is both extremely challenging and highly rewarding. A keen, zeroed-in, moment-to-moment inclination toward interdependency regulates attention into a state of taut, active awareness that can respond with optionality: the quality of having every option open equally with the depth to choose the path most in alignment with Eros.

The mind training that OM offers in optionality corrects for the tendency to develop peak states in isolation that do not translate into relational reality as well as the perception that the mundane experience of life cannot contribute to peak states. In OM, we focus on finding peak-state consciousness in connection. This vertical consciousness is the capacity to first enter the Erotic state—which will be marked by a sense of presence, a feeling of timelessness and connection to all things—without any thought. We then begin to build our lives outward from that state—one stroke at a time—until it becomes the whole of our lives. We learn to experience the feedback loop of reciprocity through the practice of OM until it becomes the way we relate with the entirety of our lives, until we achieve what is called unconditionality.

Unconditionality is the ability to meet and find this resonance with life such that the higher-order states of consciousness—love, freedom, Eros, peace, creativity—are available to us irrespective of conditions. When we can find this resonance irrespective of the stroke we receive in an OM, we can abstract it and find it irrespective of the conditions in our lives. This develops a mind that is resourceful, resilient, subtle, and receptive. OM realized is the liberation of attention that makes available an unconditional intimacy with life.

37.
PEAK TO GO DOWN, GET MORE POWER, AND GO HIGHER

While the *acquisitive mind* imagines life can be an unlimited, upward expansion of more and better, higher and richer, the Erotic mind knows otherwise. Since the Erotic mind is aligned with natural law, it lives with the truth that what goes up must come down.

In OM, there is a point in stroking up where an experienced practitioner senses the next stroke will be less sensational than the last. This sense is felt through a swollen fullness, as if we are at the end of an inhale and there is no more space to take a breath. The Erotic mind knows there is no pleasure in forcing an inhale beyond its limits, in continuing up beyond the point of highest sensation, no matter how exhilarating the journey had been up until that point. Instead, this point is the place to peak, the place at which to stop and change directions.

After this point, a downstroke is experienced as relief, as it is with every good exhale. Concurrently in life, an experienced practitioner knows to pause an upward journey before it becomes out of range, turning downward instead. Fearing failure, loss, and shame, the acquisitive mind may protest, but the Erotic mind welcomes the opportunity to empty us out.

Emptying out takes the form of letting go of the excess weight of resentment, attachment, expectation, and fear. This is known as right-sizing. Whether we welcome right-sizing or we protest, the process is going to take its course; any delusion acquired on the upward journey is then squarely released as we hit the bottom. What is left is reality.

This is where the power of choice comes in. While the child's mind may choose to meet reality with a victim consciousness in protest, the Erotic mind chooses to meet reality with approval. The result of that approval is power, which is the exact element needed to go higher on the subsequent journey up. This is the brilliance of the natural cycle of Eros.

38.
GO IN THE DIRECTION THE SENSATION IS GOING

OM expresses in alignment with nature. Rather than working against reality, OM moves with it. This moving with reality is the source of its goalless quality. OM is no more attached to going up than it is to going down; OM recognizes all directions, and even no direction, as inherently perfect. There is delight in the exhilarating, light, expansive quality of up, and nourishment in the thick, dark, weighted quality of down. Rooted in approval, the Erotic mind gives up any attachment to which direction is occurring, instead finding willingness to go in the direction the sensation is going.

Approval is key. An undeveloped mind adds resentment, judgment, superiority, inferiority, doubt, shame, and a myriad of other "extras" to the experience. The developed Erotic mind, in contrast, rooted in a trust of Eros and in a recognition of perfection, will move in the direction of flow with loving equanimity. This applies to our own experience of going up or down, as well as to when we are with someone else and they are being moved up or down.

OM is a practice of sensing for which way life is going and then discovering how to align with life. The developed Erotic mind moves in flow with loving equanimity because it trusts the natural intelligence of experience—that we will gain any necessary power, nourishment, and insight if we are willing to follow sensation rather than fight it. It knows the quickest way through is through. It's a matter of elegance. So when the developed Erotic mind finds itself falling, it turns fully toward the experience of falling, allowing itself to fall while regarding with curiosity any accompanying fear, doubt, grief, or anger.

When the developed Erotic mind sees another person falling, it doesn't run to save them; it doesn't try to lift them up, make them feel better, or in any way cut short their experience. This goes against all of our cultural conditioning of trying to be a "savior," as well as against our conventional ideas of compassion. But why would we cut short another's visit to the richest, most nourishing location of life? The developed Erotic mind gives itself over to and even puts itself behind the direction that is unfolding.

WORKING WITH HINDRANCES

39.
INTRODUCTION TO THE THREE DISTRACTIONS

Because the drop from consciousness into the body is the most difficult challenge people face in this life, many distractions come along the way. In OM, it is key to understand that the deepest fear in female conditioning is the arising of real power, a power that overtakes her and shifts who she thought she was.

Interestingly, a perfect complement to this exists in the conditioning of men, rooted in the idea that there is a finite amount of power, and were a woman to be fully in her power, it would diminish his own. This fear leads to the next conditioned idea that what makes a woman attractive is her lack of power and the fact that she needs him or that he can rescue her. It's as if she is small, frail, and delicate, especially if this is coupled with the idea that she therefore needs him specifically. The power of the conditioning is compounded in this way, and the liberation that true OM can bring inverts and tightens the bondage of conditioning, making it that much stronger.

The simplest way to know whether the bondage has been tightened is if we find ourselves thinking about the person involved, rather than the sensation, during or following an OM. A true OM will liberate consciousness into a process of purification; a conditioned OM will magnetize us in relation to another person, thus holding conditioning in place that would have been threatened by a true OM. Rather than looking for a partner who doesn't employ conditioning or punishing one who does, the key is to continue to only focus on what liberates, which is the sensation between the two partners. At the very least, this keeps us from getting snagged and instead we dissolve the threads of relational conditioning. At best, our clarifying energy becomes so strong that our partner chooses to drop into the body, and then both partners can experience greater freedom.

A woman who has not dropped her consciousness into her body is tight. The tightness is uncomfortable, but we must make sure we don't take, or allow for, any shortcuts in relieving the discomfort. The only way to relieve the discomfort of tightness is to offer our consciousness to our body. Ultimately, we don't want to be an accomplice to anybody evading their own relief.

There are three main distractions that strokee conditioning will employ as she evades real power: sweetness; and if that is seen through, protest; and if that still fails to move her stroker, brokenness.

40.
SWEETNESS

The strokee may attempt to seduce us by adding in a sugary layer that causes us to feel "special." If we, as the stroker, feel a sense of being special during an OM, know that it's a smoke screen: energy she should instead be employing back into her body is being used to distract us. If we feel anything other than a clarifying presence, pay even further attention. If the OM causes us to fantasize about the future or "more," know there is a matched amount of energy in the strokee that isn't being aimed toward her own body.

An optimal OM is one that draws us pristinely into the moment, into the stroke, with no residue. Residue is a leap into an imagined future—or a replaying of the past. In an optimal OM, there is no me, no you, no room for "special," romance, or sexual intrigue. This isn't to say there is no room for non-localized and profound sensations of presence, love, and dark richness. In an optimal OM, we are so drawn into the current moment that we start at the lowest bar.

The instruction here is to become a clarifying force by focusing solely on the point of connection between our fingertip and the clitoris. This is an opportunity to shift the center of gravity of attention from one of the most powerful lures of identity—our specialness—to the location that will dissolve this and replace it with the only thing that can actually gratify.

The idea of "special" in OM strengthens the bond of identity, much in the same way eating sugar creates a craving for more sugar. Specialness is the source of craving itself, driving our identity into more activities of bondage in order to get its hit of empty calories. Soon, both partners have sold themselves over to this identity of special and now have nothing to offer one another but the behavior that maintains it.

The one way to beat this particular identity is to meet in the field of sensation that dissolves all identity, including the sense of specialness. Afterward, we may not get that "hit" of feeling special, but at the very least we keep our Erotic dignity intact. In the best-case scenario, we become an agent who liberates the one we care about. We exchange the illusion of special for the truth of liberation. No matter what is thrown at us, we can beat the identity of special by focusing on the flow, or lack thereof, of sensation in the space between the stroker and the strokee.

The ultimate OM relationship is one of sympathy between partners. Here, there is a desire to take particular care of the other's well-being, not in a personal way but in appreciation of the other person who is so dedicated to their own and our own liberation they forego the lures of personality for each partner's mutual benefit. They are willing to be an agent of love to the extent they will use all their resources to liberate rather than to trap. It is a longer, slower, deeper route, but it proves to be the only truth that exists when we look at what true care is.

This type of relationship does not need to declare itself, nor does it need to be worked at or supported. The natural attraction to those who free us, even from themselves, is what calls us back. In this type of relationship, we throw into the fire even the places where we convince ourselves we are operating cleanly but are not—those places where we sneak under the radar. The aim isn't to be good or to confess. We have discovered that the only truth, the only care, the only relating that truly exists is that of liberating ourselves and each other. Everything else is fuel for the tumescent mind.

41.
PROTEST

Protest often comes when specialness cannot take root and often occurs as a cold front of contrarianism. The strokee has decided to use the OM as a method of complaint, categorically dismissing every stroke as inferior—either verbally with a never-ending train of adjustments or nonverbally with her loudly withdrawn attention. Though she may be adding performance on top of the withdrawal, her contribution to the OM is absent at the level of sensation. If we feel inept as a stroker then we can know she has not fully surrendered into her body. This is not to say we, as a stroker, are not responsible for ensuring the quality of our attention is strong, stable, and connected; our technical skill does contribute to the potential of her surrendering to her body. However, the humbling truth is that only she can make the choice to drop in. It can seem from her inner-wrestle—expressing as frustration, irritation, or disgust—that there is something for us to do.

The lesson here is that our skill as a stroker is dependent on our capacity to be with the experience, without feeling compelled to do anything other than continue to stroke the clitoris. Part of her protest may be the withdrawal of sensation altogether. In that case, we stroke for what it feels like to stroke with no sensation between our finger and the clitoris.

We have one other option, and this is to stop stroking. We can simply say, "I'm not feeling a lot here. I'm going to stop the OM now. Let me know if you want to try this later." The challenge is not to punish but also not to appease. We will want to do both, and the way through is to simply focus on the sensation between ourselves and the strokee. But if we appease or punish, we reinforce the behavior, and if we ignore, withdraw, or block, we also reinforce the behavior.

This may seem like a no-win situation, when in fact there is the opportunity for a big win. The big win occurs when we build steady attention in the face of protest. As a result, we develop an unconditional kindness which cannot be taken from us. This is not a performative version of kindness, but a real version.

The only way to build steady attention in the face of protest is to stay firmly rooted in power. Power is located in the neutral location of sensation between finger and clitoris. We keep that spot open with our attention and relate to the spot, not to the person. We cannot afford to relate to the individual without the mediator of the in-between sensation, or else we fall into the personal, which appears as doubt in ourselves. Having lost our center, we will get lost in attempts to prove to her we are right or expressing anger at her anger, which ultimately leads us to punishing her. But when our attention stays on the sensation, we stay informed in real time of what is happening, which gives us the power to respond consciously.

42.

BROKENNESS

Having gone through this process of presenting machination after machination, the strokee often exhausts herself and, if she is still unwilling to surrender to the body, will feel powerless and come into the OM looking for power. We must remain alert so we don't fall into the role of rescuer and try to "save her from her pain." We may notice we feel powerful, as if we could somehow save another person from their wrestle with their own life. Nothing will save her from her pain other than her surrender to her own body. In fact, everything else, including the idea of saving her, will only prolong and contribute to her pain.

Rather than the sensation radiating out in the Erotic state, it will—in its diminished or low-power form—come out through angst, tightness, grief, or tears. In the face of this, we must focus only on the sensation between the finger and the clitoris; if we focus on ourselves, we may become puffed up as we seek to help or save her, and if we focus on the strokee, we become drawn out of our center into pitying a perfectly capable woman.

It is key to remember the strokee is absolutely capable of making the choice to offer her consciousness over to her body. She is in no way broken or incapable. Her discomfort is a result of a choice she has made, not a misfortune she experiences.

In order to exaggerate our own sense that we are needed and capable, our savior identity may fool us into believing the strokee really is incapable. We must not fall for this trap. If we do, her primary means of accessing our attention will be by becoming ever more powerless as we work harder and harder to "fix" something that cannot be fixed—because it was never broken in the first place.

If we tip off our center and buy her incapability, we will feel at the mercy of her powerlessness or we may judge her for it. Instead, we must stay in the middle, at the point of sensation. This burns out our own tendency to tip to either side. It's possible that when she sees we will not tip, she will choose to drop into her body, where inexhaustible power awaits her.

43.
TAKING COMFORT IN SUFFERING OR HEALING

Beneath all the hardened complaint we hear in our heads is the softened desire we feel in our bodies. Beneath all hurt and fragility is powerful, resilient energy. When our savior archetype is activated, we may "stroke" to "save" the strokee, to make her more comfortable, to collude with her by agreeing there is a problem while perhaps even adding to the intensity of it. We fail to penetrate the delusion, because in truth she herself has not penetrated the delusion.

When we are living in a mindset of lack, perpetual opposition, or a state of defense, we cannot help anyone. We have nothing to give away. The only way to heal another person is to be seated in our own perfection: we can see the perfection beneath the perceived problem, the resilience in the person we are working with, and the truth that the only thing to do is connect and allow what is stuck to flow.

Saviors seek to fix, using resolution or fixity, when in fact the solution is the exact opposite. The solution is to open space for the dynamic process, shifting from the fixed perspective on a problem to the dynamic perspective regarding an obstacle in the play of life. When we come together with another person to agree that a problem exists and that one of us has been wronged somehow, we each fasten that perception in place, which does a disservice to both of us. We may get the temporary reward the tumescent mind offers, but it comes at a great price.

A good friend, rather than offering comfort, the collusion that exists in the dualistic world of blame, and resources for us to stay in our suffering, instead offers their attention as fuel as well as a reflection of the truth of our perfection.

We can stroke somebody in a conversation, much like we can stroke somebody in an OM—by asking them a question or sharing an observation. When we ask a question without any agenda, with the intent only to discover what is most true for the other, we experience genuine intimacy. We can likewise respond to a question with reception, or we can obscure, reject, and refuse to look where the question lands inside of us. When we stroke in an OM with an agenda or a particular outcome in mind, we can expect a loss of intimacy. If we speak to someone with a certain intent, we will experience that same disconnection. Every conversation can be thought of in terms of an OM, dynamically shifting, depending on the skill and Erotic development of each partner.

These principles Eros follows can be applied in conversation between friends—using the same terms of stroker and strokee—as well as abstracted down to the OM experience.

Attention Rather Than Pressure

In OM, we say, don't push for an outcome, such as climax, an epiphany, or a resolution. Instead, apply attention and see what wants to arise, recognizing the "problem" is a result of fixity, and represents a lack of flow in the system that has a person stuck.

We can do the same in a conversation, seeking the spot of connection and flow in simple ways such as by saying, "I notice when I put my attention on you, I feel X. Is that how you feel?" Attention can reactivate the flow, moving us into whatever dimensions a person wants to go through, whether that be anger, sadness, or confusion. Rather than trying to solve a problem, we can add our attention until it is loosened. To add attention, we simply name the feeling that arises for us. "Do you feel angry?" "Do you feel sad?" If we cannot track a feeling, we can say, "What are you feeling?"

We focus on the very moment, without any attention on the future, in the same way we focus on a stroke in an OM. What we discover is that when we are able to fully feel the experience we are having right now, an entire world of wisdom and solutions reveals itself. When the other person is expressing what they feel and the expression feels true, we keep stroking with a verbal bread-and-butter stroke, simply saying, "Tell me more," to increase the flow.

In an OM, when we are the stroker, we increase our attention by drawing it farther down into our body, asking ourselves, "What am I feeling in my belly? What am I feeling in my legs? What temperature do I feel under my finger?" We continue to increase our attention on the spot and on the sensation in our body, while using a lighter stroke on the clitoris.

When we are the strokee, we can expand our aperture. As our attention narrows in on our clitoris, we may begin to feel everything dilate. Our attention needs to stay with this dilation. We ask ourselves, "What do I notice as everything is dilating? What temperature do I feel in my pelvis?" Continuing to focus our attention on what we are feeling in our body moves our attention further into the body.

Nothing Extra

The tumescent mind has a tendency to collect problems like Velcro. While we aim to be a healing force of connection, we may get lost in sleight of hand, distractions, or panic. In OM, the focus is always on the point of connection; there may be a whole variety of movements, irritations, or sounds, but the focus remains on the point of contact.

As we work on this in conversation, first and foremost we sense what will initiate a connection. Will the connection involve sending an offering of warmth, or a receptive quality of listening? Will it be a firm pressure that calms, or a light pressure that affirms? We are not trying to solve a problem, we are trying to find connection; the issue is always tumescence and the solution is always connection.

Instead of allowing our attention to be dragged out by a focus on content, we focus on the connection that, when activated, turns the lights on for the other person. Then they discover either there is no problem or the solution has been revealed and the power to carry out the solution has been activated.

All healing happens from this place. Words are an overlay that comes as the outgrowth of Erotic connection. It's vital to recognize when we have this power to offer and when we don't; if we are not turned on, we aren't in a position to be a healing force for another. Tumescence loves to scratch an itch by "fixing." Tumescence will go in search of other people's problems to scratch that itch—it will even dig for a problem. This isn't a position of power. A powered position is one where connection feels good. There is no direction it has to go in, and we feel spacious.

In an OM, when we are the stroker, the key is to focus on the point of connection between the finger and the clitoris. This helps to remove attention from everything else. Do we feel a strong connection? Or does it feel like it's hard to sink into the spot? We are looking for the "locked-on" feeling of connection between our finger and the clitoris. Nothing else matters.

As the strokee, we bring our attention to the clitoris. We drop all movement, noise, extra breathing, and the temptation to give our stroker approval, as all of this is extra. We bring our attention instead to the point between our clitoris and the finger, until we feel the connection lock in.

Take Responsibility

Eros expands and includes. How we choose to respond to the unfamiliar defines our boundaries and the boundaries of our Erotic range. When we choose to expand and include the unfamiliar, whether it is a sudden surprising desire or the unexpressed anger of a loved one, we are challenged and privileged to reach beyond ourselves. We are called to respond from wisdom beyond our experience. Naturally, fear and scarcity may arise, and even this is an opportunity to expand and include. As we do so, we grow more into who we are, beyond our preconstructed identity, and beyond our individual conception of who we are.

We cannot persuade another person to expand their range with us as we talk to them, but we can do everything in our power to set the conditions to facilitate that they can more easily choose. We will be able to feel where their consciousness is grooved to reject instead. If they continue to do so, we can stop the conversation. If we are feeling irritated or frustrated with the conversation, we can and should bow out. Otherwise we may try to override our felt sense in order to get an outcome from them, likely using pressure.

The ins and outs of our own triggers are crucial to know. The tumescent state is like a heat-seeking missile whose aim is to get us on its ride, subtly trying to activate our reactivity to bring us under its sway. If we are triggered, rather than trying to work it out in the background of our mind, we can say aloud, "I got triggered."

This sounds deceptively simple because people often assume the stroker position is "doing to" another, and is hence invulnerable and impenetrable. In fact it is the opposite; the stroker position is deeply connected. If we become triggered, we are sending that into the other person's state under the radar, where the communication is actually happening. Our vulnerability is our power as a conduit of healing. Our stoicism is the insensitivity that will have us stroke for a result.

The strokee will try to use rational mind tricks, such as referencing an authority or professional who backs their opinion, remarking that other people believe similarly, or stating that science proves what they are saying. They may try to hide behind vague opinions from a third party.

If the strokee is unhappy and perceives a problem, the tumescent mind has taken over. We have the option of stopping the process, and in this case we must also be careful we don't fall into a problem-oriented mentality. This kind of mentality looks like believing we are at the mercy of the situation, that we don't have the option of turning on to where we are, and that we don't have the option to leave.

In an OM, when we are the stroker, our focus is completely on the most turned-on spot. If our mind drifts away from this spot, when we notice it we can say, "Checked out." Speaking our present state aloud is a way to bring ourselves back to the present moment. We begin to notice what has our attention moves away from the spot, such as our partner's noise or lack of it, her turn-on or lack of it, or her requests and adjustments. Whatever takes us away from the focus on the spot, we say it aloud briefly in the moment and then return to what is happening at the point of contact.

As the strokee, we must be mindful of where we try to take our stroker off the spot. Where do we distract as they draw nearer to the spot? Do we adjust just as they are drawing near? Do we move them off the spot by making certain noises? Where is our attention as the stroke draws near to the spot?

Peak

We may get stuck in a circle where someone wants to keep running over the same content and doesn't want to open into something new. In that space, we can feel their grip. An urgency may arise on our part to do more. Instead, take a break. Allow the strokee's desire to build again. Simply say, "It sounds like you are happy where you are."

When someone pushes against us in conversation, or we sense the sensation is decreasing, we must remember the volition of every person. We are all where we want to be, and we can lift our attention from the conversation. Over-stroking—doing more work than the other person—creates a dependency. They have the solution within them; we are merely stroking for it to rise to the surface, not to insert our own.

It can be difficult in the throes of a heated conversation—where the person is arguing for the problem or insisting they are unable to simply stop some behavior—not to try to show them the way out or prove something. The art of turning our attention, or changing the subject in that moment and letting the tension of the peak decrease, builds a relationship where both are equally sending and receiving.

In an OM, as the stroker, we change the stroke the moment we believe the next stroke will be less sensational than the last. We then find the next spot of highest sensation, or we lighten the stroke so the clitoris comes out with the desire to meet our finger.

As the strokee, when the sensation has lessened, we can push out slightly through the clitoris, allowing the spot to expand and open where it naturally wants to go next.

Penetrate the Energy

In a conversation, if the strokee is in the spinning form of tumescence where they can't cohere their thoughts properly and may be acting erratically, it's our purview (if we have permission) to penetrate the tumescence. Truth is the verbal form of Eros, so we state the unfiltered truth of how we are experiencing this person—not what they should do, but how we feel in their presence. We may have a tendency to speak indirectly and with judgment, however, communicating directly and without vindictiveness is a way of creating resonance. To meet someone with solid pressure in this spot allows them to come down.

By speaking the truth to people as we see it, without filtering, we connect our essence with their essence, and the tumescence can be dissolved. The tumescent mind of the other will try to bribe our ego into doing the work for them, our payoff being we come away feeling like we're more powerful than they are. We must stand up to the part of them that would obscure the answer from themselves, but not because we were ego-bribed to do so.

In an OM, as the stroker, when we are unable to get on the spot, tumescence is often the reason why. We increase pressure slightly, with the intention of our stroke going down. As a result of aimed attention and increased pressure, the tumescence will decrease, and the spot will reveal itself.

As the strokee, whenever there is tumescence, we put attention on opening. Internally saying, "yes," helps open any spots that are closed.

Secure Our Part of the Feedback Loop

Just as a strokee in an OM secures her pelvis to ensure she does not "lift off" and only go on the stroker's ride, the stroker should remain centered in themselves. In a conversation, we take in the experience of another and allow it to flow through us without going over into their experience. We maintain a perfect, resonant, and dynamic tension. If we instead get carried away by the content, we will lose our capacity to be a pole that allows the energy to flow between both partners.

In an OM, as the stroker, we center ourselves in our seated position, feeling our butt on the cushion. As we put grounding pressure on the strokee's legs at the beginning of the OM, we stay in touch with our own body and notice what it feels like. We keep our ambient attention anchored in our seat, as well as lightly on what we are feeling in our body throughout the OM.

As the strokee, after we are in the nest and feel the back of our pelvis on the ground, we anchor ourselves there and place our attention on our pelvis, keeping our ambient attention there throughout the OM.

Maintain Openness

If we focus on anything other than the connection between our partner and ourself, a connection which allows us to stroke for greater truth and realization, we may try to direct the strokee's experience toward our own preferences, thereby shutting off their experience. We may wind up having a radically different experience from our partner. Remember, if we are able to get behind their desire, whatever it may be, we both will ignite. We stroke for what is most resonant with the strokee's body, revealing their truth rather than attempting to direct it.

At the same time, it's important to be honest as to where we are unable to stay open in the face of what is being said to us. It may clash with our personal hopes in a way we cannot get beyond, or it may not align with our ethics. The instruction is always to focus on the point of connection, but if this becomes impossible, we should stop the process. We don't want to secretly angle, manipulate, or direct someone based on our viewpoint. The stroker must take great care that the strokee does not try to stroke from the bottom as a way of not letting go of control, seeking to know "our problems" or wanting to "feel our vulnerability."

In an OM, as the stroker, if we can't find the spot, we may feel a tendency to get upset with the strokee. This immediately takes us out of our center. Instead, we should drop lower into our body and feel for any stroke that lights up our fingertip, then stroke that spot.

As the strokee, we allow our desire to be felt in the OM. This doesn't resemble fantasy or seduction, but rather our genuine desire, which is often shy and wants to emerge. By allowing our desire to be felt, the stroker can then find the spot, and the OM will ignite.

Attraction

We may feel disturbed by the unambiguous nature of Eros, which operates with clear lines of attraction or repulsion. If we are not feeling a true attraction to stay in the conversation, we should immediately stop. We are not obligated to force any kind of connection in order to be a good person; if anything, we are required to stop so as to not over-stroke. At the same time, if we are energetically called, we must answer—even if, to the rational mind, this looks like a burden. We aren't answering to idea-based rules, but to attraction and repulsion, both of which are cut and dried. The action may look the same, but the source is entirely different.

We take care not to block or cut another person's tumescent mind. The tumescent mind will feel it has a "one-up" position. It will try to use duty-based rules to get us to act against the truth of what we feel, telling us we "should" be open, loving, welcoming, or accepting of the other person's behavior in order to be righteous or good. But in Eros, righteous or good means honest. While we don't owe anyone anything, Eros will often ask us to give in places where it is against our preferences, and not to give in others where it is against our preferences. Listen to Eros over tumescence.

It's important to remember that the body and mind want to heal. Healing is contagious: we can have so much Eros that others catch it. But tumescence is also contagious. It's vital to know our mind and where we might get hooked into another's tumescent story. Do we fancy ourselves the only one who can help people when no one else will? Do we see ourselves as a rebel, so they hook us into a game of "us against them"? Do we look for external approval so we can feel wise? Are we insecure about our attractiveness, so we give up our peace of mind for a compliment? Tumescence is challenging to work with.

In OM there is no force. As the stroker, our only aim is to feel whatever is present in this moment, using value-neutral attention. Is connection present here? Are we on the spot? Is there turn-on? We stroke to find resonance with what is.

As the strokee, we need to be present with what we are feeling in our body. There's no reason to block, make ourselves bigger, or hide during an OM. When the finger is on the spot, allow it to be felt. When it isn't, simply be with it.

44.
HOW TWO SENSITIVITIES ENGAGE

Finding resonance with another sensitive person after there has been a snag in the connection can be a particularly challenging instruction. To engage here goes against much of our conditioning toward withdrawal as a form of testing another to see if they "care" or will "come after" us. We get snagged on the other side of the equation as well if we believe we demonstrate care for another by going in after them, appeasing them by taking on responsibility for not just our part in the snag but theirs as well. This instruction offers an uncomfortable honoring of free will.

Eros honors the fact that people are capable. If they are not finding joy in engagement, it means they are choosing not to. If they are not coming toward us, it means they are choosing to be distant.

This is an acknowledgment of perfection and volition: things are as they should be, and true desire is demonstrated by attainment. True desire allows others to be how they are and choose the path and circumstances they wish. Even if they look miserable in their choices and communicate that they are stuck in them and have no choice but to remain stuck, they are actually making the choice to have no choice. A fundamental respect for desire is needed along with an acknowledgment that desire is dynamic and needs space to work.

In an OM, when we are stroking, and the clitoris is withdrawn, a desire may arise in us to do the work for them. We may press in to reach the clitoris, which communicates we are willing to soothe the strokee and take care of them. But if we do, we reinforce the idea that our partner is incapable and that we are unwilling to sit in discomfort while they make the choice as to whether they wish to come out.

We have several choices if the clitoris is withdrawn. One choice is to match the action; our partner has withdrawn the clitoris, so we can pull back the finger a bit. This also works in the other direction where the clitoris can match the action. In either case, we are giving our partner a choice. The key is not to be retaliatory, stating: "You've withdrawn, so I will withdraw, too." The idea is that by withdrawing, our partner demonstrates their desire against all of our preferences. Their desire and our preferences are often at odds. The work of OM is to give priority to desire—the felt and seen direct experience—over how we would want it to be, and to use energy for desire instead of in an effort to impose our preferences upon another, or upon life.

By withdrawing our finger, we are instead asking, "Okay, how is it?" Then we assess how it is, demonstrating through our stroking that we listened and are willing to match what is offered to us and reflect what we hear. This communicates (in spite of any retractions, frustrations, or constrictions) that there is nowhere we need to get to but right here. The way out of discomfort of the spot isn't to abandon the spot, but to be with the spot on its own terms.

Our mind may want to turn this into a trick in which we hold our breath and stay with the spot, hoping it will change. This tendency is just the nature of the mind. (The good news is the spot likely won't open, so we will get to practice even more.)

If we choose to pull back our stroke a little, one of three things will happen. The clitoris will retract even more, likely as a means of testing whether or not this is real and whether we are trying to trick it into coming out. The clitoris will remain exactly as it is. Or, the clitoris will come to meet our finger, which is a sign we have built trust.

In OM, as in life, trust is built one stroke at a time. Using bread-and-butter strokes will help integrate new trust. The mind may instead want to "make up for lost time," speeding ahead and getting fancy, which will likely cause the clitoris to retract. Or the mind may want to retroactively punish and now increase pressure, almost grinding in the process.

If we can lock in the moment that the clitoris meets the finger, using a bread-and-butter stroke until the clitoris offers a deeply lit-up spot to guide us to the next place, we are good to go. If we have experienced a retracted clitoris that comes out in an OM, and the rest is bread-and-butter, we have created an extraordinary rewiring of trust. More OMs will follow; we can afford to take our time. The more time we spend, the more solid a foundation we build for the relationship. More importantly, we reprogram the hungry, goal-oriented part of the mind to be here right now, with this stroke, as it is.

Should the clitoris retract even more, we have two other options. The first is to again match the pulling back until there is the slightest contact, even if it feels as though we are just stroking the lube. This may seem like the OM is not happening, but in fact it is happening at a deep, trust-building level. From this we are communicating. We will remain in connection as long as it's physically possible without violating the choice being made. This is the total reversal of having an agenda; in OM, through an agenda we either fail to notice the choice somebody has made or punish and withdraw. Instead, this option is a subtle and rare act of kindness to the self and to the partner. It undoes the reactive nature of what we may feel inclined to do when one person withdraws.

If we cannot maintain contact, it's best to lift our finger for about two seconds, breaking contact with the clitoris but maintaining contact with the thin layer of lubricant, then place it down on the clitoris again. If the clitoris is still retracted, one way to proceed is to safeport our partner and end the OM. Again, this cannot be done as a form of punishment. We are replacing personalities with resonance, and the resonance is what we are responding to, not the individual. Our intention is to stay in resonance no matter what. When we do this, we are free of the influence of tumescence, free of making and forcing, free from taking withdrawal personally, from needing to assert our will if withdrawal is seen as rejection, and from withdrawing in reaction. If we stay in the neutrality of resonance, we remain open to master those conditions and not become prey to the tumescence of another.

This resonance buffer allows us to operate in true kindness. We now have enough space between activity and response to choose an Erotic response. For example, withdrawal communicates a lack of trust, which, at the deepest level, communicates a lack of internal safety. To feel anything other than compassion for a person who feels unsafe isn't Erotic.

What each of us does with this understanding is entirely up to each person. We may determine this isn't a good partner for us to OM with at this time, since we may feel we cannot let go, considering their unwillingness to trust. Or we may determine this is a great opportunity to learn to slow down and be with someone who doesn't feel safe. Or we may determine now is not the time to take action, and we will wait until we feel a natural pull back to that person. The resonance buffer gives us room to drop down into ourselves, feeling for the most on-the-spot response.

One thing to point out here is that, in OM, hovering or energetically not penetrating (when permission has been pre-negotiated) on either side constitutes deliberate withholding. The instruction is that if we are able to meet the stroke, we must. Many people only understand boundary transgression in the world of appearances, where it's more tangible and palpable; OM gives us a lens to address transgressions in the invisible realm as well. To deliberately withhold when we have the ability to meet a stroke is an aggressive act aimed to provoke further aggression.

In the world of appearances, we may look perfectly innocent, even able to give the impression we've had our boundaries transgressed, while simultaneously transgressing other people's boundaries under the radar. OM gives us the capacity to tune in at this unseen level to see whether the withholding is due to a person's genuine inability to meet a stroke, or an act indeed intended to hurt.

On the other hand, sometimes we may sense from the clitoris, or from the finger, a pushing that communicates a demand, a right, an entitlement that extends beyond the point of resonance. In that case, there may be a sense from the clitoris that there is an agenda; perhaps there is a drive toward climax or to add in a sexual flavor, coupled with overt aggression. The OM isn't open and spacious, nor moving in accord with the underlying rhythms; the same may happen with the finger.

It should be clear that in OM, this kind of scenario can arise on both the physical and energetic levels. We get caught in the physical, assuming everything is happening only between the finger and the clitoris—but OM is energetic. We might also fall into the mistaken idea that OM is unidirectional, as if the stroker alone is doing something to the person being stroked. But the person being stroked has as much impact as the person stroking; when the intentions of both are to find resonance, the OM is open and "on." When an agenda takes root on either side, the energy becomes closed off, reduced to the merely physical. The OM then seems "fixed" in the physical.

The challenge when there is an over-assertion of energy is our tendency to over-assert in response, or even to collapse our energy. But this takes us out of our buffer. Remember instead that we are not *not* reacting for their benefit, but for our own. What then happens here is a very subtle trick: the way we avoid stepping into feeling put upon by an agenda that feels like pressure, or that is reactive and invites meeting it with aggression, is to increase our energy and attention in a value-neutral, balanced way. We increase the "send" signal of our energy. If we are stroking, we make our stroke more deliberate, using greater focus (not necessarily greater pressure), as if we were throwing a fastball in baseball. The energy rolls off the finger in that manner.

At the same time, we are receptive, deliberately absorbing the agenda in an effort to drain it from our partner. This action is a perfect match of power and approval, involving neither collapse nor aggression.

We never leave our sphere of approval. The second we start concocting a story about how our rights have been violated, we are out of the power of our sphere of approval and communicate that we are powerless. We internally communicate that we cannot match this energy and are at our partner's mercy. But this is never true.

All sensations can be met. If sensations can be met, so can feelings. When feelings can be met, there is steadiness. When there is steadiness, whatever the world delivers can be met. More importantly, what can be met does not need to be fought, blocked, or punished. This differs from the cycle that exists in the world of appearances where instead of meeting whatever is delivered, a sense of powerlessness and punishment is thrown back and forth.

Meeting is the antidote. Matching what our partner offers us in equal measure without anything extra is the way.

Matching our partner communicates that we will not let their reactivity set the direction of our interaction, nor will we let our own do the same. Instead, we will find resonance and meet our partner there. Should a partner turn away from meeting us, we don't chase them, and should they want to return, we don't punish them. For there to be resonance, we must relinquish the entitlements and rights of our own preferences. We don't get to determine how our partner responds or force our partner to respond in any way. To do so would take us out of resonance. If they are being aggressive, we can still find resonance. We need neither to bow nor fight, but to meet with a firm attention, powered enough to remain approving—not of our partner per se, but of what is occurring in the timeframe.

We get to remain here in resonance, regardless of what may be thrown at us and what may be removed. This freedom is brought by matching what our partner offers.

No one is obligated to do anything when we land upon the baseline of sufficiency. Anything offered is a gift, which is the language of the body and the language of desire. The body doesn't respond well to obligation or expectation. The conscious mind may contort and demand we respond in a certain way, but the body does not abide with the sensation of joy. Instead, we let the body lead and make offerings—or not. We allow others to do this as well; no one owes us kindness, sympathy, or attention. And we do not owe these things to anyone. Obligation kills the potential for coming from a genuine place.

What do we do with our feelings when another person doesn't show up, match us, or meet us? People coming from the world of obligation make demands or shut down. We have no need to do either. We are not at the mercy of another's response, and if we interact with what's happening in the moment instead of with our expectations, we are free. Everything else is extra, including the hurt, the anger, and any other responses. Those experiences, the everything else, are outside of the spot. The spot is an ever-dynamic, shifting location, while those experiences are fixed. And while those feelings may occur inside of the spot, they occur as part of a much larger whole we don't need to fixate on. This is where we get drawn into sentimentality or anger, into the idea it should be different from how it is.

The only thing that ever "hurts" is our inability to meet a moment. Every moment met is beautiful. Notes of pain may play inside the moment, or even sharp notes of rage, but these are experienced as part of a larger movement. To feel sentimental is not to feel at all; it is to rise up into the mind, disconnected from the body, and endlessly play out images in our head. We isolate one note, play it again, and again, and then act from that limited place.

Don't do that.

Instead, let it all be immersed in the larger pool of sensations and distinct, dynamic moments. This is how we can each feel while never denying reality. It's how to avoid getting stuck in attempts to control reality from the disembodied tower of the mind.

When someone moves away, it's skillful to move away in response. This is our way of saying we acknowledge their desire and movement. To give more than is requested, even when the requests are invisible or energetic, is an act of arrogance. Even if that act may look kind, generous, or benevolent, it's actually an insult to the other—and will bring about a shame in them that we have assumed they have been unable to do what was required for themselves. The meeting in resonance of friendship holds space for others to do what they are capable of, as well as for us to offer what they are not capable of, when this has been requested or when we have received their permission. While it's acceptable to oversee another person's nervous system when they seem locked or frozen, this must be done with their agreement. True generosity is meeting another person's desire on their terms. This is neither a self-aggrandizing act that helps us feel good about ourselves, nor a transgressive act to assert what we perceive they need.

We must watch closely that we don't do for others what they themselves are capable of doing. If we do, we render them incapable. While they may at first relish what we have done, the unused energy in their system will turn into a self-hatred that will then bleed onto us. We may sit with them while they learn, but we must not do it for them.

45.
BENEATH THE FOG IS EVERYTHING

The most challenging channel to open is the non-registering or non-confronting channel. This type of stroke is one we cannot track, but we know it by the irritation and confusion it leaves in its wake. Perhaps it's too subtle or in a direction we have never attended to. It may be on an inactive spot. In OM, the aim is to awaken 360-degree attention, including all spots, all directions, all speeds, and all pressures. Waking up means finding fluency and resonance with each and all.

An uncomfortable truth beneath not tuning into a stroke: every stroke registers in the body whether or not it registers in the attention. The stroke is happening, being felt and experienced, but it is simply not being tracked; information is entering but is being filtered out before we can register it.

This gap is the result of the tumescent mind believing itself to be separate and isolated, wanting to maintain its dominion, and thus filtering out anything that would threaten it, or at the very least not support it. The filtering process can then run amok to the point where we have absolutely no idea what's happening in our own internal world. What we don't address controls us. The whole world is still happening, but we are not there for it. Still the body remembers everything.

To the extent we fail to confront a stroke, a choice that takes more energy than actually confronting the stroke, an "ignore" charge builds up. The charge may build to the point where there is such a fog that when we get up from an OM, we can scarcely remember one stroke. Or in the midst of the OM, we may find ourselves so locked out of the body we don't register any sensation.

This non-registering attention is a means of protection, a mistaken idea that the way not to feel discomfort is to disconnect from the body—like anesthesia, where surgery happens and the body remembers but the mind does not. Then the whole process of recovery (which is happening in the body) makes no sense, and we have a feeling of always being out of step with reality, as though something is going to come and get us.

Our life continues to happen, but we aren't going along with it. We wake up in shock at all that has happened. In this scenario, we feel as though life is happening to us, but if we would have stayed with it, it would have happened in direct proportion to what we were capable of knowing.

46.
MEETING OUR EROTIC SELF BENEATH THE FOG

Profound potential exists within the dense fog of confusion that occurs when we don't confront a stroke. The fog signifies we are hitting a foundational layer of the filter between mind and body—a separation that attempts to split life into our own arbitrary categories. However, reality isn't divisible; it is the ignorance of this that undergirds the repulsion and the grasping, along with our attempt to devise a pain-free, "pleasure-full" reality. Any charge that fails to be filtered through rejection or attraction has a final safety net where the encoded instruction is simply, "Ignore." A thick layer of confusion and unknowing collects. The instruments of sentience and perception become clouded, and we become dense.

It's hard to track this tendency because, when we're in denial, we cannot know what we fail to sense. The instruction here is to focus on the fog, using our attention like sunlight.

A stroke will happen, and instead of the clarifying wave and wringing-out sensation that come with resonance, there is a deadness as it falls, like a thud. Lock into what an "on" stroke feels like. The ambient attention can always keep this in the background as a running comparison. This prevents us from inhabiting the fog and doing its bidding, which is to go off into rejection and attraction. The ambient attention to an "on" stroke also communicates to our deeper sense what's possible; it sets a due north.

Dense fields require more powered attention than thin ones. Due to their difficulty, they carry an implicit suggestion that we look away, avoid, or even collapse our attention into hopelessness. Instead, we must simply continue to watch the fog. This is where steady, non-hovering, and noncoercive attention is vital, since the opposite characteristics increase the fog. We hold and observe.

We will then notice something miraculous. Densely concentrated thoughts, feelings, and emotions (everything we avoided in the past) will arise from the fog, as if an entire life that had been concealed all along is emerging. What we might have considered numb or checked-out was in fact densely packed material that had not been digested. As this numbness begins to come alive, we may want to follow the threads. Instead we must continue to watch. We are waking up a spot. It's as if we are melting snow, and life-forms buried beneath are coming back to life.

But we are not done yet. Another layer is beneath this. As we continue to hold our attention, we find a ground underneath: a location beneath what we know as ourselves. We may feel like we fell through a trapdoor and our identity got stuck up top. Devoid of the structures that hold the ideas which make up who we consider ourselves to be, is only a pure sensing—a sense of liberation from a prison, a sense of no longer being bound by a set of arbitrary laws. This is optionality.

Further beneath this lie the jewels. We may sense this layer as something familiar, yet something we have never known, like a voice that has bled through the walls, sometimes clear, sometimes muffled. It occurs as a force, but a force so familiar it brings with it a sense of unimaginable safety, a sense of knowing beyond what we have understood knowing to be. We sense that seeing itself can be inhabited. We see from source into source. It is impersonal while simultaneously deeply personal. It is unassailable, a knowing that, when integrated into consciousness, has us understand the benevolent reason for every interior instruction ever received. The rejection, the grasping, and the ignoring all fall away—not because they are bad or even because they cause pain, but because they simply dissolve into this force.

In OM, this state is called apotheosis. Apotheosis is what climax seeks to be, what climax tries to achieve by going up and over and crashing into the body—a place where what would have been climax going out inverts and brings us down. The nervous system locks, and the momentum acts as a ballast against which the tumescent mind lacks the power to resist. In and through the body, we are brought to the "down" we have avoided our whole lives. But sometimes consciousness from this place is too exhausted from the fall to receive the wisdom. In this case, the body serves more as a hospital in which to recover than the ground from which everything issues.

This moment is when we have allowed consciousness to descend far enough into the body that it can connect to the gifts that come from below—gifts that can only be known in the act of offering. We offer ourselves for this state of possession, in which we are held beyond what we can look away from. Our seeing now heals the wounds created from previously not seeing. Our knowing now heals the wounds from acts previously done in ignorance. We are meeting our Erotic self, the force that will guide us into the totality of being beyond good and evil.

OM MASTERY

47.
THE ADVANCEMENTS OF ATTENTION

One of the many gifts OM provides us with is a pristine reflection of where we are in our practice. When we are honest with what we are perceiving, we can discern through OM how we use our attention in any given situation.

In a single OM, we are able to travel through any number of landscapes of experience and observe how we respond to them. We see where we feel steady and alert, where we get stuck, where we have optionality, where we become rigid, where we feel irritated and reactive, where we feel easeful and flowing, where we withdraw, and where we become aggressive. OM allows us to see in great detail where we have learned to harness the power of our attention, and where we have not yet harnessed it. OM shows us how we operate with ourselves and others, as well as how we navigate the sensations of life.

The Advancements of Attention illustrate the progression of how we can use our attention, and what might be needed for us to reach the next level.

Desire

Our attention is passive and easily distracted, but there is an underlying, quiet inclination toward connection. More attention is spent on internal dialogue than actually feeling the stroke. Staying connected requires great attention.

Curious Attention

As we begin to feel the point of connection, we feel a flicker or buzz of electricity in our finger. Our desire to feel is slightly stronger than our fear of pain, and fear of pain keeps us from entering into the realm of the Erotic. Latent fears may arise, but we become aware of how much Eros we have.

Some common thoughts enter at this level and can hinder us. We may hear a voice of fear that feels powerless saying, *I'm just being used for my finger. I'm never going to get this right. I'm never going to get mine.* Or, a voice that is afraid it cannot please might say, *I'll never be able to find a stroke she will enjoy. I can't make her happy.* Or, a voice of fear that believes there is a scarcity of goodness for them might say, *I don't care about the container or what she says. I'm going to make her like my stroke.* Greed sets in, and we go faster and more intensely than the energy of the OM itself.

Trustworthy Attention

As we feel an incontrovertible electricity in our finger, we can now rely on our ability to locate the spot. We feel a distinct difference between on and off. Our attention shifts from *performing* to *feeling* as we begin to relax into the stroke.

Flow Attention

We learn to allow electricity to move through our finger, as though the finger is being moved. Having discovered the point of electricity in the clitoris, we develop and adequately sustain enough connection that electricity activates equally in the stroker and the strokee. A feedback loop develops, forming a circuit, the first place where we feel the involuntary.

Fearless Attention

The direction of the stroke is no longer determined by our preferences, and we do not decide which strokes our body receives with gusto. We are moved instead by where the most sensation is, and because we are moved by the most sensation, an uprooting occurs. We can locate where we are, even in seeming groundlessness, and we have the confidence to face our fear that we ourselves are not doing the moving or responding. A deeper thing is moving through us; the feelings are more natural. We begin to open our spot.

Active/Volitional Attention

As our finger rests on the clitoris so the spot opens, we develop the ability to add power to our attention. The attention now becomes stabilized in an active position and is strong and supple, enabling each stroke to be distinctly and clearly felt. This state is where we are awake and have volition, which requires our active attention to remain "on" the whole time. We begin to feel every single stroke.

Powered Attention

We don't feel resistance to any stroke. A marked experience of effortlessness as well as a dynamism feeds our capacity to stay connected with any stroke's direction, speed, or pressure. In the face of increased intensity and subtlety, our attention remains steady. We don't get stuck on opening a single spot. We begin to volitionally open other spots, allowing what feels good to open.

Transmuting Attention

We learn to transmit and take in energy from all. The attention has been purified to the extent it is transparent without being pushed or pulled. We begin to stroke back with our clitoris. It becomes impossible to tell whether the clitoris is stroking the finger or the finger is stroking the clitoris: union and stillness—union in an untested way.

The Erotic State as the Full Realization of the Erotic Impulse

The Erotic state is now defined as a state of consciousness marked by a sense of connection or intimacy with all things. It begins with the original *Erotic impulse*, followed by the full activation of this impulse, and then the unimpeded opening of the involuntary. Consciousness can now surrender to the body, and a true OM begins.

48.
THE THREE LEVELS OF OM

The lowest level of OM is a clear mind that doesn't grab on to any particular thought. Thoughts move through just as debris moves in a river. Feelings and sensations move through us as rhythms but remain dynamic. We are able to maintain steady attention on the point of connection between the finger and the clitoris. We are also able to maintain attention on the stroke without our attention moving toward the past or future.

At the level of physicality, as if a light has been switched on inside the body, the rhythms play through it. When the lighting turns up, our physical experience becomes more buoyant; a light or warmth emanates from within, with a feeling of expansiveness. And when the lighting turns down, a charged darkness goes inward with a deep, calming density and a sense of being enveloped.

This internal lighting changes as if a skilled hand is moving a dimmer switch; the shift is seamless. Our body becomes so fully inhabited, saturated with the experience. We can still sense the physical, but at a much more refined level: we sense the groove of the fingertip or the smallest bump on the clitoris.

The second level of OM has an openness and dynamism that moves thoughts through us without force. Feelings and sensations become palpable, as if our nervous system is composed of keys and our sensations are playing them.

We experience a full, round beauty to all sensation. Nothing occurs as discordant. The key to this level is that the transition from one sensation to the next is experienced with a throughline of joy. Every note of sensation is played through to the end with no holding on as one sensation transitions to the next. Every sensation is welcomed as refreshing and necessary.

Feeling tones play through our sensations, adding richness, though these feelings are not personalized in any way. What could be called sadness is experienced as a dark, rich timbre. What could be called anger is a bright electricity. What could be called lust is a dark, warm, orange, pulling sensation. With no static self for the sensation to adhere to, the notion of coming back to that kind of static place is unattractive. The only truth that exists is a raw, pure sensation that can be felt by feeding the static self into it—not the other way around. Simultaneously, our body experiences greater concentration and saturation, as if we were inside our own cells.

Level three of OM is a radiation of clarifying light, alternating with an absorbing darkness. The stroker and the strokee exist inside of these until this alternation occurs, and the OM is no longer about "me" and "my partner," as if the OM is breathing us. All movement and stillness happens through us, and we are liberated together into this place.

We execute nothing personally. A new relationship with our body emerges, where we are so inside our body it becomes everything—an almost unbearable feeling of something akin to gratitude and a saturation so concentrated, like we are within the heartbeat of life, with a sense of a "coming out of it." As if we have been inside the truth of how things are and where they operate from. With this new awareness, the world of appearances looks radically different.

The mind has now been clarified and nourished. What looked stimulating or pleasurable before seems pale compared to this simple, rich clarity. What used to bring us the greatest pleasure seems empty compared to what we know is possible. We do not make ourselves stop our previous pursuits; they just fall away because they are dissatisfying. Level three is marked by the infinite nature of "here" with no desire to go anywhere else. We need no nirvana, vision, or height to ascend. The everything of this moment ends all searching.

THE EIGHT STAGES

49.
LEARNING THE EIGHT STAGES IS LEARNING TO FOLLOW THE BODY

The Eight Stages are dimensions to become intimate with, rather than stages to be attained. If we are hoping the stages will all line up so we can ascend the ladder, master them, and graduate, we will be sorely disappointed by the Erotic journey and by life itself. The Eight Stages are more like waves moving through; we never know which dimensions are washing in and which are moving out, or where we will find confluence. The aim is to become one with the waves, to have a pitch-perfect response to every shift and change, and to recognize where we are in each moment.

Strength of attention and strength of response are required for us to remain in the deep, eternal, ever-connected state of the Erotic mind, even while conditions continuously change. The Erotic mind requires no special conditions to exist.

Eros faces the truth of constant flux head-on. Rather than allowing us to merely observe the waves, Eros throws us into them. Sometimes we learn by being pummeled and going under. On rare occasions, we learn through something inside of us waking up that allows us to move with the waves exactly as they are.

When we study Eros through the Eight Stages, we learn how to follow the body, discovering it knows precisely what it needs, with a self-organizing intelligence always operating. Following this intelligence through realms that terrify, mesmerize, alarm, fulfill, and soothe, it becomes life; it does this by being truly lived.

The study of the Eight Stages begins with climax because our culture is so climax-addicted that the art of climax has never been truly considered. Climax can be used as a means of clearing karmic baggage, of polishing the sense instruments, and (most importantly) increasing and harnessing stuck energy rather than blowing it out and depleting it.

An advanced practitioner starts at climax with all the signifiers of climax—parasympathetic activation, contraction, swelling, lubrication, and a clear, empty mind—the moment a finger goes down. We continue there as long as we desire, with climax becoming a way of life—a consistent and persistent practice of discharge that counteracts our human tendency for acquisitiveness. When we experience other kinds of climax in life—when something in our personal life explodes—we tend to perceive it as punishment. But in Eros, climax is both the reward for and the evidence of a good and diligent practice. Climax is the offering of and the opportunity for an initiation, bringing us beyond what we think we can do; it is the test and proof of all prior practice. If we make it through, we experience unimaginable freedom. If we fail to make it through, we experience unimaginable bondage. Climax is the signifier that we are ready either to release into a new level or to return to the beginning.

Each of the Eight Stages is a necessary realm of exploration in our journey to understand our own wholeness. Some of us may assume we know everything there is to know about some of the stages, when in fact we haven't even opened the door to them. Other stages that we consider quite advanced and out of reach prove to be beautiful, but with overly self-important gateways.

If the Eight Stages teach us anything, it's that there is and there isn't an ultimate state. Exactly the way things are *is* the ultimate state.

50.
INTRODUCTION TO THE EIGHT STAGES

The Eight Stages lead, like doorways, into various manifestations of the whole of consciousness. At any point, we can land in any stage and move backward or forward. We experience the stages in OM and they may reveal themselves as dimensions making up the broader experience of life.

In Eros, an underlying principle is that truth is a throughline of congruence. The abstract and concrete coexist in a mutual system of checks and balances. If an idea cannot be brought down to the physical, or abstracted into the absolute, it's questionable. This makes our body and mind effectively the laboratory in which all research is carried out. We seek for the throughline and release ideas that pull us off our search, concentrating on the ideas that correlate.

Through this process we can tap into universal and unique truths concurrently. Words refer to something specific. Take, for example, the word "cow." The actual animal is the referent for the word. Then there are abstractions, ideas that contain the original referent, but with fewer specific details. "Cow" may go into a collection of likenesses such as "livestock," which can then go to the next collection of likenesses minus certain details, which we call "animals." These can become "farm assets," "assets," and then "wealth."

When we can follow a line all the way down from the high-level abstraction of wealth to the physical reality of a cow, and carry the physical reality up to a high level of abstraction, we call this an *Erotic truth*. This kind of truth is dynamic while also reflecting an internal order that can be examined. We understand a dimensional reality, rather than a merely linear one, by seeing the congruence across levels of abstraction. This is how Erotic beings operate.

When we mentally walk back through our experience to test for proof, we discover we are not stuck at the ground (or physical) level of reality, unable to abstract into the deeper dimensions of the body. We also do not get stuck in the higher-level abstractions, where our abstractions relate to only other abstractions but are completely disconnected from the physical level.

The Eight Stages fasten our understanding of experience across all the abstractions of life. As we learn to inhabit them, they become further abstracted into healing, connection, liberation, and purpose. Our heart-based, mind-based, and soul-based experiences with family, relationships, and work reveal that they all operate according to the same basic laws, but may play out at different levels.

We may expect, or want, to progress from one stage to the next, moving sequentially from the density of climax into the ever-more subtle aspects of stillness. But life does not work like that. Eros does, however, provide the opportunity to attain equal facility on all levels. It reveals that, while many of us live at levels of greater density, few of us have great facility there. In Eros, the ascent and descent as well as the travel between the two—the stability, smoothness, and suppleness of the movement—are all of equal importance. We can develop acumen in each of these.

Eros aims to have us inhabit the whole of reality equally in all directions, with equal reverence for all its aspects with no presumption that one is more sophisticated or more worthy of our aim. In the world of Eros, this arrogant perspective is most likely driven by ignorance, by an incapacity to see the interior wisdom of a particular realm. It's easy to dismiss a realm when we are holding it against the perception that another realm is higher; we assume the higher realm is better—a goal to be attained. The secrets within the lower realm cannot be seen with that particular eye.

51.
THE FIRST STAGE: CLIMAX

A flooding beyond the point where we could pull it back.
Backlogs of tension wash out and, in their place, comes intuition.

Brought down
Release anything false
Land in the Soul
Taste the real that will reorient you

We typically think of climax as "having an orgasm"—the result of an internal impulse activated when we exceed our capacity for sensation. This type of climax strives to restore a balanced state of sensation, to bring us back into equilibrium. We fasten our attention onto a goal—to the exclusion of all else. Anything not aligned with this goal is perceived as a disruption and must be ignored. The body is forced to produce sensation surpassing its normal thresholds, with the mind seeking more from the body than it naturally provides. This particular kind of climax is an attempt to pump for, and forcibly extract, a few moments of excessive pleasure at the expense of the harmony and ecology of the body.

The mind knows two modes: control through restraint and control through excess. In the natural, spontaneous expression of the body, this control dissolves. The climax impulse is the most dramatic of these spontaneous expressions, therefore we must employ the most extreme form of self-will, either in avoidance or pursuit.

Too limited to encompass the seamless whole the body naturally inhabits, the mind must focus on singular aspects that either avoid pain or promise pleasure, leading to either constriction or driving toward. The mind holds its own agenda front and center, forcing the body into compliance. But when this force of climax is held in the fullness of the body, it roots us in a kind of power and we open beyond what we are capable of closing against. When held within the body, climax allows us to see more, feel more, and know more of naked reality.

However, when the force of climax is fixed in the mind, the opposite outcome arises: fixation occurs, locking on, discharging beyond our capacity to stay conscious, and eventually shutting down. This force becomes the ultimate tool for greater ignorance, advancing an agenda that uses the resources of the body in ways that bring harm, not only to the body but to the felt sense of unity the body offers. Control-based climax mutates into a weapon wielded against unity, fracturing our natural ecology.

In this scenario, we conflate Eros with climax, and climax with the rapacious drive that's activated when our mind co-opts this force. By extension, we associate Eros with the negative outcome of its misappropriation, swinging between avoidance of the Erotic field altogether and the massive effort required to control the climax impulse as we attempt to prevent a discharge.

What is intended to be the ultimate vehicle in the play and interplay of the naturally arising, seamless nature of reality instead becomes the reverse: *habituated* climax, the type of climax we are familiar with. Habituated climax is like smoking—if we hope to find relief, repetition is required, allowing the craving to build up until discharge is inevitable.

In habituated climax, we experience only a fraction of what Eros has to offer. Rather than sinking into our body more deeply and embracing our sensations more fully, we discharge surplus Erotic energy—energy that is in excess of our customary levels. We do this in an effort to return to our comfort zone, to homeostasis. The buildup of stimuli results in anxiety and discomfort, and we expel the accumulated tension through climax.

The result feels less like fulfillment and more like relief. We get a brief, superficial kick that returns us to where we started, or even below. Rather than a dam breaking open, we are temporarily unclogging a drain. In and out, over and done. This kind of climax may meet our basic needs, but it does little to bring us into the depths of Eros. It may blow off steam, but in no way does it blow open the mind.

Most people are conditioned for habituated climax. Muscles tighten and genitals grip in response to moments of high sensation. As a result, Erotic energy gets locked into tiny, constricted spaces, where it gathers until it eventually bursts forth. Because it is so intense, so cataclysmic, the urge for climax has a way of drowning out the subtler notes of desire. With our muscles clenched and our attention elsewhere, we remain a prisoner of our habituated grooves for needs-based sex, keeping us in a needs-based consciousness. From this place, we have a fixed goal that determines all our preferences. We use pressure, avoid phase transitions, and over-stroke in an attempt to reach our goal.

On Preferences

Habituated climax looks at climax as an exercise in repetition, focusing exclusively on experiences that are "supposed" to occur during climax—*climbing* and then *going over*. Like swimming laps, habituated climax has a limited range.

Non-habituated climax, by contrast, makes use of every note on the piano. Non-habituated climax includes the full symphony of feeling that Erotic interaction has to offer. In non-habituated climax, we are willing to enjoy every available sensation without preference, and therefore are never hungry for Erotic connection. We can draw gratification from any stroke.

In habituated climax, however, we hold tightly to preferences, relying on a certain kind of partner, position, and circumstance in order to activate. For this reason, we are constantly longing for another opportunity to climax. Each time we empty out, we immediately start craving the energy we just lost. Because we only activate from the small handful of sensations we deem appropriate, we are consigned to long periods of hunger. Like a predator surrounded by the wrong prey, we don't take advantage of the abundance of sensation that's always available. Were we to see, approve of, and integrate what is already available, we would be inside of non-habituated climax, but in habituated climax we hold out for the strokes we like best, even if it means starving.

Phase Transition

A phase transition, like ice melting into water, then boiling and evaporating, is not linear. A simple shift into the next state, there is no single moment, no violent unlocking. This is the movement of energy in OM.

We may shift into the pure release of non-habituated climax, but it is smooth, not jerky or rocky. This is because in OM we inhabit, rather than gloss over, each stroke, which is a radically different approach to life. We allow ourselves to have all of it and then, when full, to be moved to the next stroke. We remain at peak sensation.

Pressure

In habituated climax, pressure is applied to force activation. This kind of pressure is a type of weakness that comes from a lack of power. In non-habituated climax we find power in allowing, rooting our attention in precisely what is happening and recognizing that no goal, no concept, could be more important than this moment.

When we root our attention in this way, a magnet builds inside us that draws in precisely the right stroke. This cannot happen in the starvation occasioned when we are in habituated climax, seeking relief. It comes when we are able to liberate fullness from the craving engendered by habituated climax.

The magnet inside us grows stronger and stronger, drawing in precisely what matches it until a seamless response exists between what we are yearning for and what we are having, all self-organized by the magnet within. A phase transition, rather than an expulsion, occurs at the point of fullness.

Over-stroking

We remain at peak sensation when we neither over-stroke nor grasp. Over-stroking occurs when we find pleasure in a location and stroke beyond its capacity to continue to deliver fresh sensation. The pleasure initially comes from having found a location that's packed with charge and, as we stroke, the charge begins to move, and we feel an electricity in the body. Over-stroking begins when there is no longer a charge, but we refuse to move or look elsewhere. At this point we apply force to activate what little charge is still left.

When a spot is fresh, we can feel how alive its magnetic charge is by barely skimming it. We are stroking for this field and our finger, like a dowsing rod, is seeking this. But over-stroking is the grinding sensation we feel when we get into a rut of a stroke. Our attention has collapsed or become intoxicated by the initial charge. It digs in rather than moving toward a new location where charge is fresh and abundant. Our unwillingness to face the window of not knowing and uncertainty that may arise when looking for a new location with charge locks us into the diminishing returns of an over-stroked spot.

Transitions

When disconnected from the body, the mind would rather know mediocrity or numbness than face the potential for aliveness that can be found through a transition in uncertainty. Only the body-trained mind faces uncertainty well. This mind develops sensory acumen so well it is bestowed with a skill level that is increasingly certain. At the master level, having been positively reinforced as a signifier of new spots to open, uncertainty becomes the home in which our attention is most comfortable.

The attention, rooted in confidence from having searched and found the spot so many times, has achieved wealth. The goal of skill-based confidence, which once drove the mind, has been met; it now stands on new ground.

From this foundation of confidence, we can enjoy the luxury of the wealthy mind—a mind that is no longer trying to overcome the poverty of proving itself to itself. Now our mind can take risks, get lost for the thrill of it, and explore unknown territory.

Sensory Discernment

The promise of practice is that what previously occurred as an obstacle now occurs as a thrill. A new world opens up. We no longer need to guzzle down sensation; we can stop and note its qualities. We can afford the sensation of wanting, because it is a *felt* sense of wanting, no longer based in sensory starvation. We discover that the mind can track sensation with such sharpness and precision we can note the exact moment a single charge goes off in any stroke, feeling the body heat and thaw with the climax of each stroke.

Previously, in the centralized experience of habituated climax, at best this occurred in the genital area. The sensation would spike for a few moments into the other areas of the body, only to descend lower than it was prior. But now, with our attention on this moment-by-moment discharge, we feel as if our entire body liquefies, and something altogether different takes place.

Apotheosis

The state immediately prior to discharge is the rarefied space of true freedom—apotheosis. During apotheosis, sensation radiates through our body, clearing out any stagnant energy, with self-perpetuating, purifying clarity. The clarity permeates the body and, along with it, sentience increases beyond known bounds; antennae reach out into domains of experience that could not otherwise be touched. This state is a stillness on the verge of crashing, stillness like that of a tightrope walker.

Just as the string of an instrument requires the right tension to hit a desired note, apotheosis will only express within an optimal range. The order of the voluntary nestles up against the chaos of the involuntary at the gap just at the edge of climax. The sweet spot that exists in the in-between is where all that is stuck is liberated. Lying between comfort and grasping, this is the location from which gratification radiates.

Non-habituated Climax

If the body has liquefied, and climax has been liberated from the grip of control, when the climax impulse activates, a sense of unimpeded rolling takes with it every last bit of anything stuck. We can sense our awareness, too, is liberated, flooding beyond the point where we could pull it back. Because the body has been erotically stretched over time with sensation, it is able to allow for this swell without any contraction.

We sense the climax is not contained in the body nor in the mind, but rather, both are contained inside this charged, sentient force. In contrast to the catapult and crash of habituated climax, non-habituated climax continues to roll until it lands us on solid ground. Rather than leaving us with a sense of depletion, we experience it as energizing, because there are no violent throes to exhaust the body. Instead of raging like wildfire over the surface, non-habituated climax reaches into our depths of bone and sinew, emptying out any tension-creating impurities. The mind is absorbed into these new places in the body, into a deeper sense of knowing—so rather than experiencing simple relief, the mind expands and becomes more complex. Backlogs of tension are washed out and intuition rolls into their place.

Thus in non-habituated climax, two primary characteristics have changed: through stillness we have grown our capacity to be in the fullness of sensation, and we have reduced impurities. As a result, each cycle of non-habituated climax makes more energy available to push out into the world—in contrast to the habituated version, which is solely based on depletion.

In non-habituated climax, no dramatic expulsion offers the seeming relief of emptying the "trash," because we have already been releasing energy. The trash has already been emptied, and consciousness (in this case, rooted in the body) can radiate out, unimpeded, to touch the furthest reaches of reality. As much as the mind can stay tethered to the body, the body will permit it to explore. We have no time limit or distance limit—only the question of how secure the line is between our body and our mind.

When our body senses the connection may snap, it draws the mind back in. This is why habituated climax is a few short seconds, like going to the symphony and only hearing the cymbal at the very end. Habituated climax stops right where it might otherwise continue, were the yoke between the mind and the body more secure.

If climax is a lightning bolt, non-habituated climax is an extended sheet of lightning. We don't open our eyes; our eyes are opened. We are simultaneously flooded and emptied.

Climax Demands Our Surrender

Surrender is required to experience non-habituated climax. We surrender our fixation on climax as a goal, our unconscious mental and physical habits, and our attachment to our homeostatic comfort zone. Stroke by stroke, we enter the realm of the involuntary, fully engaging with every sensation, rather than passively accepting sensation.

By cultivating a deep capacity for surrender, we develop a fluency with the involuntary; we are able to have a lava ride that roars through us, clears us out, and takes us into ourselves.

Climax in OM

When we are in climax in OM, we feel as if we are overflowing with Eros and out of control. Often, a falling or exploding sensation occurs. The physical release is in direct proportion to the amount of energy that was made volatile.

When we are turned on in climax, we feel as if a dam is being unleashed and we are fully integrated into its flow. Effortless, rolling over, expanding, and building energy, we are left feeling soft and energized. The experience is mind-opening and consuming; we feel full and wrapped in a thick, honey blanket. To have this turned-on experience of climax, we first need to develop the skill of surrendering to sensation, which involves giving and taking light strokes as well as navigating resistance. Physically, this also sets the bar for an involuntary ride.

If we are turned off in climax, we are in habituated climax—efforting, pulling, or pumping to make a release and expulsion happen, as if a drain is being unclogged. Climax is the phantom that's always being chased; without it we feel lost or disappointed. The physical experience is either drastically numb or painful, like glass shards. Afterward comes a feeling of depletion. When we are stroking a partner in climax, using a consistent, bread-and-butter stroke (medium pressure, speed, and length) makes it easier, as the strokee is climaxing, for her attention to latch on to the strokes. While the stroker initially agrees to be the strokee's object of projection, something her attention can latch on to, eventually, her attention develops enough to be fully located in her body. She can then lie back and truly enjoy the experience. But, if the strokee knows no stroke will help here, she should inform her stroker and end the OM, releasing them both.

52.
THE SECOND STAGE: RESOLUTION

We come face-to-face with our own raw, pulsing heart.
We allow ourselves to be touched by the realization and promise of Eros.
This is our home.
Instead of rendering us weak, it's where we draw our strength.

Washed out
Forgive to heal
First taste of our authentic value
Source of genius is revealed

Following climax, waves and paroxysms move through the body, shuttling our consciousness in a bottomless descent. In the habituated state, this descent often ends in anxiety or sleep. It lacks the necessary gravity to make it down into the true reward of emptiness: the experience of an essence that lies below the protective walls constructed from our deep-seated fear of being hurt.

The force of Eros can break through, cracking the walls around the heart constructed by pride, indifference, aloofness, hysteria, envy, and comparison. We glimpse something untouched by the infractions and aggressions of life: something naked, vulnerable, and innocent. We come face-to-face with our own raw, pulsing heart, allowing ourselves to be touched by the realization and promise of Eros. We see that what we have viewed as our weakness—a place where an inexpressible homesickness issues that we think we must escape from or conceal—is, in fact, our home. We draw strength from this place that we have viewed as our weakness.

The throb we previously experienced at a distance, through protective layers, proves to be the direct throbbing of our heart when touched in nakedness. Through climax, Eros washes away our protective layers, allowing our mind to move down into the very center of our lives. As long as our attention has been purified of the tumescence that would have it buoy back up, it can sink in and release its confusion and lack of knowing. Our consciousness is able to let go of what it has been holding on to in its attempt to protect us.

We rest inside of a knowing deep enough to hold the whole of us, from our worst badness to our inexpressible, paralyzing yearnings. Finally, someone has us. As is the way of Eros, we are now faced with ourselves and with the burn of seeing how we have hidden, run, blocked, or demonized the delicate nature of our heart. We feel as if we can hear our own heartbeat from the inside.

Even as we want to turn away from this, we are surrounded by a forgiveness beyond human understanding. We sense the work is done, that all Eros ever wanted of us was to come home to our heart and allow Eros to come through. We are humbled as we see our efforts were unnecessary, and that our only work is to return and reside here. Eros seeks itself and lives in this truth.

As we rest in the heart of Eros, we learn how to receive the world just as we are received by Eros—with relief, joy, gratitude, and celebration of our return. There is no need for Eros to forgive, because no crime has been committed; getting lost and forgetting where our home is has been our only transgression. Even our defiance against home was in truth a forgetting. Eros embraces us and holds us, the only appropriate response to one who has been lost.

If climax is flooding, the stage of resolution is *welling up*—gratitude, relief, tears. What we call an "afterglow" is our heart welling up with love.

Yet there is an emptiness to it, as we find we have confused emptiness for lack and felt a need to fill. Stilled from the outflowing of climax, we find we cannot return to our habit of acquisition and filling, as we have learned our best adornments are not nearly as elegant as the nature of the heart. The hope is that in glimpsing this beauty, something in us is reversed: instead of simply drawing in, we can also allow outward flow, thus living in an unfettered heart showcasing the natural beauty that can only be seen rightly with it. When seen, this beauty is so breath-giving, we resolve to live with openhandedness. Our resolution is not out of generosity; it's to release anything that would obstruct our view.

The most terrifying place in Eros is the virginal mind resolution brings us to. Self-consciousness has been absorbed, as well as the need to be the best dog in the show, always repeating the same tricks. We return to ourselves as we were before all the cunning defense mechanisms installed themselves in our mind. This is the pure, alive moment when we realize everything we thought we knew is wrong. We realize we are useless to Eros.

We now have two choices: we can head back out to the limited world and look good, or we can allow ourselves to be vulnerable on our knees, the only place Eros can reach us and begin to work through us. With this second choice, the power of wonder is restored, and it is a power. Think of the world-weary suitor who is undone by the virgin, and consider who holds the power in that dynamic.

Eros Enters the Erotic Heart as Love

In the resolution stage, there is a sensitivity to the clitoris and the finger in OM—a sense of burning often associated with pain. We might presume neither want to be touched, when in fact they want to be met with the most exquisite attention.

No motion is required and, when contact is made, essence knows essence. Here is knowing without preconception, without filter—a renewal, a rebirth of the senses. Free of the leash of concepts, this sensing organ delights in the curious exploration it yearns to do.

The wall between the mind and the body has been knocked down by the force of climax, and now, mind and body are brought together and exposed. Ideas that previously operated as the enemy of the body play through the heart as inspiration. With the barrier between them removed, the yearnings of the body that so threatened the mind are able to add power to its ideas. As these two forces come to see what can only be seen through a heart that knows they are better off for the other's existence, the body fills with a sense of being in love.

However, in habituated resolution, we may not glimpse this prior to passing out. We may feel a sadness we can't quite locate, or we may lock up to prevent the unknown descent. That which wanted to be washed away may instead circulate even more through the mind, likely in the form of shame or self-recrimination. This fundamental mental shame views itself as having failed for losing control, and becomes determined to redouble its efforts to restore control.

If, instead, we reclaim our birthright to descent, we can go even further down. As we descend, we may experience a seeming numbness. However, just as a black hole is not the absence of matter but actually an incredibly dense concentration of it, this numbness is not a sign of a lack of sensation, but rather of its superabundance. This impacted sensation indicates we have too much for our sensory apparatus to process all at once.

Here, we often resort to theatrics rather than slowing down to feel all of the sensation. If we instead tune in, we see our own power of gravity to draw in. Eros enters the heart as love. Previously, our heart was full of the hatred we created inside ourselves as a way to protect against perceived external hatred. When Eros enters, it demonstrates the truth of the home we are coming to inhabit. We are healed by this love filling our now-Erotic heart. And this is not at the expense of our genius; it is the very source of it. Here, we have access to the wisdom of all things by the leveling of identity to the location where we all meet.

Resolution in OM

When we are turned on and in the resolution stage in OM, we are tuned into subtlety and relish rich and nourishing sensations. Our nervous system feels bathed in these sensations as we resettle into our body. When we are turned off, we feel either sluggish and heavy or overly sensitive in a way that communicates we do not wish to be touched. This stage feels like an unnecessary waypoint where we don't want to be and we may find ourselves checked out.

OMing in resolution requires a precise attention in order to feel this new set of subtle sensations. With this attention, we recast the down as honorable, offering unconditional approval. Inside our preconceptions of pain or sadness, we find the sweet spot of rawness.

When stroking someone in resolution, we stroke with a stillness to receive her outpouring of energy, sometimes stroking with such light pressure that we are merely stroking the lube on top of the clitoris, not the clitoris itself. The resolution stage has the most heightened sensation of the down stages, yet the sensitivity does not mean the OM should end. Instead, we make space for the down sensation, which may manifest as tears and an energy of grief.

If our partner is turned off, we should have her verbally direct the entire OM, while keeping our finger receptive to draw out sensation rather than quenching it. Over-stroking or using too much pressure at this level of sensitivity could result in disconnection in this stage where there is the most potential for connection.

When we are being stroked in resolution, if we think the sensations of down are shameful, we may disconnect from our clitoris. The invitation in resolution is to give ourselves permission to be felt in this location. We maintain a level of engagement to add gravity to the downward movement, rather than merely sinking in and riding it. We allow the sensation to prickle with the light strokes, which keeps the sensitivity alive as those prickles collect, pulling sensation down further. Making requests here keeps us from being self-sufficient. If we find ourself turned off in resolution, we push out our clitoris, feeling one stroke at a time, and adding attention to each. We find one good stroke and communicate it to our partner.

53.
THE THIRD STAGE: RESTORATION

From emptiness we develop a world in which the senses can rest.

Cohered back into a self
Rest in the truth of Erotic pleasure
Stay with the sensation
The wisdom of the body is revealed

Most of us are familiar with habituated pleasure. When we are hungry, we take pleasure from eating. When we are tired, we draw pleasure from rest. When we are tight, we discover the pleasure of a stretch. We access pleasure through maximizing our biologically programmed rewards, such as with food and security. An anxiety exists underneath the consumption with the question, "Is this all there is?" This kind of pleasure is mindless consumption in an attempt to provide comfort to numb or insulate from the emptiness we feel in our heart. We don't realize the heart is the source of our deepest pleasure, our homecoming.

Often, we *only* know habituated pleasure, and we consider it normal restoration. It can cover or soothe our sense of insufficiency. Existing at the level of biologically or socially conditioned constructs, habituated pleasure rewards us for meeting the criteria of our biological needs and our social codes.

The first issue with this is, in a sense, we are keeping ourselves comfortable in hell: the hell of avoiding the question, "Is this all there is?" We are merely rearranging furniture on the deck of a sinking ship. Another issue is that these types of pleasures offer diminishing returns, requiring us to work harder and harder to access pleasure while receiving less in return. We swim in circles and never find the true pleasure that comes with breaking free from the cycle.

For the most part, pleasure exists at the level of the mundane: sex, food, relaxation, and sleep. But it can also exist at the level of indulgence, with a kind of hedonism that focuses our attention on the surface layers of the body, since these are the ones that cannot be drawn further down. Our attention goes to any lengths to provide an endless stream of circumstances to fulfill our increasing demand for pleasure. This kind of indulgent pleasure is rooted in bigger, better, faster, more—yet there is never enough.

To know true Erotic pleasure is a vital art on the path of Eros. Following the extreme gradients of the other stages, pleasure can restore the senses, but to truly comprehend or practice the art of pleasure is rare.

Erotic pleasure is a replenishing force. It's an invitation to elevate the senses so they can respond to the incorruptible desire, not of mere biology, but of Eros. Eros will settle for nothing less than the spot. Erotic pleasure is a call to greatness and precision in the care and tending of our body, and it also removes the cause of our discomfort: our misunderstanding that the throb of our heart must be muffled because this is "as good as it gets."

We only discover true and enduring pleasure with a heart that has been revealed and exposed following the experiences of release and resolution. Only from the resulting emptiness, with the sensing apparatus now sufficiently cleaned, is our perception clear enough to point us toward the creative endeavor of developing a world in which the senses can rest. We recognize our senses cannot rest in opulence, but only in the beauty, richness, and elegance of simplicity.

The truth about beauty is it only occurs in the now. Resting in the truth of Erotic pleasure is what nurtures wisdom. Intellect, driving the mind, renunciation, or seeking for truth do not help here; only the mind that rests in pleasure, properly nourished, will naturally reveal the wisdom of the body. Our greatness is thus birthed, not from the strivings of the mind, but from the craft of pleasure. When the eyes rest and are not strained, they see better; the same is true of the inner eye.

In OM, we access this state through bread-and-butter, medium-pressure strokes, focusing solely on taking pleasure from either the finger or the clitoris. Through softening and receptivity, we learn to draw pleasure into ourselves. Pleasure isn't something we make, but something we allow to bathe us.

Pleasure requires precision in *moving with*. Given that a pleasure-based OM is a meandering OM, it moves at *tempo giusto*—the tempo in a piece of music that feels appropriate and ideal, considering the nature of the piece and the characteristics of the notes. When we move at the tempo the sensations themselves seem to request, we get to savor the pleasure to the fullest.

The key is for us to continue to move with the stroke. Otherwise, we may fall into a pleasure slumber, settling for a complacent, autopilot experience during which our attention turns passive. Erotic pleasure is active, whereas habituated pleasure is passive. Passive attention leads to diminishing returns as a hardening sets in; pleasure becomes a right or a demand and we have a kind of "golden handcuffs" attitude where we become convinced things are good enough. Growth looks unattractive and we don't feel the impetus to change. Our attention is lax, and lax attention always carries with it a sense of dissatisfaction.

If we catch ourselves stuck in this location, we can interrupt the trance and put our attention directly on the dissatisfaction. This will add the contrast that brings pleasure back into the experience. After all, pleasure is made of contrast. The best foods are salty and sweet, and the best touch is strong and soft. We reawaken pleasure by un-fixating the mind from the preferential good.

Restoration in OM

When we enter the restoration stage in an OM, we feel as if we are filling up again. Energy is slowly building with a sweet, easy, predictable, nourishing feeling. If we are turned on, the experience feels relaxing and pleasurable as we immerse in the sensuous world more clearly and deeply than we have before. If we are turned off when we arrive in restoration, we don't want to move with the stroke; we want to stay in one location, so we try to slow down to maintain control. We have a resistance to going up.

The skills needed for OMing in restoration are drawing in, taking touch, and easing in with a bread-and-butter stroke. We learn to discern sensation again and to focus attention on the clitoris. The strokee makes requests. Developing a regular OM practice is important here.

When we stroke someone in restoration, we use gentle, simple strokes with lots of affirmation. We stroke to increase sensitivity, leaving the strokee higher than she was before. We stroke the spot with the most sensation and change the stroke at the peak. If the strokee is turned off, we under-stroke slightly so she can feel her desire. Responding to her requests builds her confidence. There may be a feeling of demand to stay in one spot, especially to avoid electricity, so we must be prepared to meet resistance with compassion. We are willing to remove our finger without punishment.

As the strokee, practicing OM as much as we want has us build the pool of pleasure that will nourish the senses. We relax and receive, and when we feel lost, we draw in. Remaining with the sensation keeps us from drifting into fantasy. We approve, request, confirm, and request again.

If we find we are turned off, we start by creating a beautiful nest. Describing the sensations aloud and vocalizing in connection with our genitals helps move us toward turn-on. We may stop OMing because we are practicing saying "yes" to preferences as a means of building a reservoir and filling up.

54.

THE FOURTH STAGE: TURN-ON

A sense of radical activation where the power is turned on.

The spell of habit is broken
Struck by a power we cannot outrun
Go against preferences
The fire that clarifies and the passion that brings meaning

In the turn-on stage, we shift our center of gravity, moving from habituated forms into true Eros. The mind has made the journey down into the depths of the *Erotic heart*, becoming magnetized to the charged space of emptiness rather than fixed to the identity. We go from seeking to eradicate insufficiency and constantly searching to find out if "this is it," to offering our mind to our body and our body to the Erotic. We tend to our body, expanding its capacity to hold Eros so it can be a vehicle through which this sentient force may operate.

We only need to make one change: to shift the fuel we use, from fear to desire, from the rational to Eros—in other words, to shift from fossil fuels to renewable resources. We do this to become clean, burning with unlimited fuel. An organic change takes place when power is readily available, when there is no lack or scarcity, and when we are not living amid our own pollution.

Our interior world is restored. The strain and effort that pass for spiritual work, the theatrics of submission, and the controls necessary for a system clogged up with pollution and operating on lack—all prove to be the circular problems and solutions of a tumescence-based world. We have been driving in search of clean air, all the while in a vehicle that produces pollution.

A unified heart understands that the rational mind exists to serve while the Erotic mind is the deeper intelligence, and not the other way around. When we are coming from this heart, we are brought into a state of intimacy, coherency, and belonging. It isn't that Eros is better; it's deeper. The static mind of the rational cannot contain the dynamic reality of Eros, whereas the dynamic quality of Eros can contain the static truths of the rational. The Mystery we aim to enter is infinite in nature, and the finite nature of the rational has only finite instruments to track reality; it cannot sense beyond its constructs. To enter and navigate, we need the proper instruments, which can be found in Eros.

Through climax, our rational mind is subsumed by our body, and its rigid structures dissolve in this deeper consciousness. Our mind may "hit bottom" in resolution, admitting with grace and relief that it's not equipped to meet the Mystery. Our mind can now surrender to Eros, and we are liberated from the search for surface-level resolution from conflict because we are now able to see through the seeming opposition. We see the underlying truth that the poles are complementary. Everything remains exactly the same, except we can now see things as they are.

From this vision, it's as if a whole world grows up. In restoration, we take the time to allow our new sentience to gestate. Turn-on issues from this gestation; yet, from here, turn-on is different by orders of magnitude from the old-guard version of pumped-up performance we previously considered it to be. Turn-on is a lightning rod through the center of our being. In later stages, we harness the energy created here into heat, light, and fire. The energy created here is converted—using our emotion as steam to move us and our mind as fire that clarifies—and wed to our Erotic impulse to become the passion that brings meaning. We leave behind that old-guard version, which was more like a lightning bug buzzing around our genitals.

The habituated mind uses all its resources to prevent this very flash that now takes over the whole of our body, mind, spirit, and soul. In Eros, our body becomes the lightning rod that draws and grounds the force. Turn-on is so often diminished or trivialized, but in fact nothing could be more important. Turn-on is the source that brought us into the world, and it has the intelligence and power to carry us through it. Turn-on is our divining rod, leading us away from that which is dead or deadening and toward that which sustains life and aliveness.

The heat of this force moving through us then activates the Eros that has been dormant in our system. What was static and fixed now flows like electricity between the poles, dynamic and alive. Disordered molecules, previously unavailable, are gathered and brought into the current, moving in a unified direction. The sensation experienced is that of radical activation where the power is turned on. Effort is transformed into effortlessness. It may seem as if we have been bestowed with something supernatural and now have access to a mystical power, but it is hardly that; rather it is our own self, turned on.

Imagine a world built by people with eyes that cannot see and who are perpetually in darkness. Imagine the aids that would seem like absolute necessities, and the methods for reading the world, or the external tools that would be required for motion. The world would be built to accommodate a deficit that didn't need to exist and as a result would be radically slower, more cumbersome, necessarily more careful, and lacking an entire dimension. Entire systems with their institutions, cultures, customs, and governments would develop to accommodate this lack.

Turn-on allows us to dispense with the extra, which is the filter of the rational we develop to bridge the distance between our capacity and the world. When our capacity is no longer limited, we either dispense with or reappropriate the tools.

Our first genuine experience of turn-on may be disconcerting. It is a moment of absolute and total possession; we are struck by the lightning we have spent a lifetime trying to outrun. This lightning occurs as the sensation and as the actual experience of an electrical arc in our body. We feel a jolt through our body at the point of connection between the finger and the clitoris, as if the finger is plugged into a light socket, electricity flowing. The jolt is too powerful for the mind to hold or control. Imagine the first jolt of habituated climax, then turn the volume up tenfold, extending it indefinitely until it is done with us. This is the experience of turn-on.

Anything static is blown out, and everything that remains is electrified; no aspect of our body fails to be electrified in this way. The lightning takes over our entire body from the top of our head down to the arches of our feet and we can hear an audible hum. We feel the blood circulating, the heart pumping—everything coursing and alive.

The finger and clitoris feel locked in this arcing energy. We see how they become circuitry, how the voltage is so high that this lock sets in, holding both partners in place in such a way we could not move even if we tried. We see it from the inside, how this flash of white has taken over both our interior worlds. What was a dark mystery is now a shock of white so bright there is only light. We feel how it holds us there, refusing to let us down. This is turn-on.

And then we feel how, if we have developed an attention that can remain with it, we can track it as it turns back down, like a light on a dimmer—the electricity incrementally dims and our body is gently released back into itself as it comes down into the nest. Without this attention, we are like a light with just an on-off switch—our body is in shock and crumples back to the nest in a heap.

We notice how our interior world looks. The light now remains "on" inside. What was once invisible reveals itself. We notice the warmth and the glow. We sense the aliveness, the buzz and hum, the release, and the bringing to life of what has been seemingly dead or numb. Latent feelings, previously painful in their dormancy, are alive and dynamic. Compressed love moves through, its movement like the music of sadness and the liberation of joy. Our interior world has gone through the death process of climax and resolution, then was held in restoration, and is now resurrected in turn-on.

This experience is life itself. This is our direct contact with the force of evolution that brings phenomena from potential to realization. It is what flows through the bud to have it blossom, what flows through the mind to turn ideas to genius, through the sperm and the egg to transform into the baby.

This neutral force, when activated, operates on phenomena to bring us ever more into what we are. The line of electricity that runs through all of life is now switched on inside us. The information is encoded in our essence, but it will also need guidance; at this stage it is operating as a primal or elemental force, carrying with it tremendous power for both creative and destructive potential. Ultimately, this force is always seeking for wholeness and a totality of being—the activation of the will to achieve humanity.

Parts of us are often rejected by the rational mind as being unacceptable, and the demands of our humanity are too often resisted. But the activation of this force brings us beyond what the rational mind is able to resist. For this reason, and because it is undifferentiated in its power, we must bring the force into the peak location of the heart, where it can be connected to the world of aim and intention.

Turn-On in OM

When we enter the turn-on stage in OM, the energetic body is waking up and will likely have an appetite. We feel electric, vibrant, molten, and vibratory with the sensation of the light going on throughout. If we are turned on in this stage, every moment of gratification only leaves us wanting more. We have the first glimpse of the orgasm being directed by the essential self. A refining happens as we find certain strokes deepen the sensation and are therefore more attractive. Organic preferences arise that are not based in hunger or conditioning.

If we are turned off in this stage, we feel dug-in and have a lack of joy for anything. A sense of unease and anxiety, like the ground is starting to slip away, and an aggressive agitation may arise, as if something is brewing just below the surface and we cannot control it. We have a frustrating lack of power or ability to maintain stability.

The skills needed for OMing in the turn-on stage are discernment, circulation, and expanding our sense of the body. We learn to discern each stroke from others. We circulate electricity throughout our body. The feedback loop between thought and sensation becomes part of our reality and we expand our energetic body beyond the physical.

When we are stroking someone in turn-on, we touch the point of highest sensation—the spot—allowing the sensation to flow through the finger. We stroke gently but persistently, both playful and gently tenacious, until we feel ignition, at which point we lock on and let it take us. If our strokee is turned off, activating our own system will generate the origin of a feedback loop.

When we are being stroked in turn-on, we expand our energy body, spreading out sensation so it isn't just concentrated in the genitals, playing at the edge of going over but without going over. If we are turned off, we approach OM as a practice, showing up to the nest even when it seems challenging. We practice saying "yes" to every stroke.

55.
THE FIFTH STAGE: THE PEAK

We have soared as high as we can soar and just before we plunge back, we can taste a serene, open weightlessness. We are pure, potential energy.

Loss of the familiar
Embrace transition, making it home
A moment extends into timelessness, apotheosis
The most concentrated flavors of life are tasted

Everything that rises must fall. Eros is no exception. In Eros, this fall is a welcome relief; we come out of the electricity of turn-on and enter the refuge of the peak. This is a time of being suspended, the feeling of the moment we have reached the apex of a leap on a trampoline. We have soared as high as we can soar. Just before we plunge back, we taste a serene, open weightlessness. We are in a bardo with pure, potential energy and a feeling of groundlessness, where all that was solid has melted. We feel as if we are moving in every direction at once. Our mind feels it can touch dimensions otherwise inaccessible, while also feeling into the depth of bone and sinew. Eros extends through and beyond the body in all directions.

Eros can go to either extreme, but it lives in this in-between, the moment at the top of the inhale, right before it turns into an exhale. Here, it is weighted and pregnant with potential.

This experience can be one of liberation from circumstance, or a type of hell for the mind that's been habituated to rely on familiar strokes or grooves to feel safe. For that habituated mind, this can be an experience of terror, of seizure from not knowing what to do, or of flailing and protest. This suspended space may be filled with anxiety and a sense of being untethered, encompassing a futile demand to return to an old feeling that's no longer there, and a desperate race to reach the next landing place.

In order to find ground, this weightlessness may birth a variety of compensations. The most common compensation is to use artificial gravity, labeling the feeling a "problem" so we can employ the tumescent mind in forcing a solution. The tumescent mind now has something to hold on to to bring it back down. It can buck against the change, blaming the partner, or it can take another tack, seeking to draw the partner in further by providing a sense of security. It can also simply blot out awareness altogether by doing the equivalent of holding the breath until a landing happens.

The moment we call the peak a problem, our OM takes place in a field of neuroses. At the same time, all of our practice is for this phase transition.

Just as the heart is not a location but rather a result of connection, our capacity to respond in a peak with volition, rather than with the default of neuroses, is the result of our prior practice. (Incidentally, there is no way to develop the capacity to respond while in the middle of a peak; this can only happen on either side.)

The peak and how we respond to it reveals our emergent self—not the self we want to be, not the self we think we should be, but the self who emerges in environments beyond our capacity to rationally determine our actions. Until activated by a situation, we won't know how we will respond to the natural impulses that have the power to take over us: anger, Eros, arousal, craving for power, fear for our lives, threats to our security. At the sensory level of an OM, even a simple shift in stroke can activate the root sensations of these impulses.

Root sensations are single units of sensation that contain the seeds these impulses would grow into. OM breaks them down to one stroke, giving the mind the capacity to meet them.

What happens at the moment the sensation and stroke change, at the height of a concentrated peak? We can conjecture, we can guess, but we cannot know. This is precisely why the peak is both thrilling and terrifying. The only way to know who we are beneath the command-and-control center of our tumescent mind is to see who we are in the peak, in stark relief.

Following a peak, an untrained practitioner may scramble to regain ground, trying to resecure the position with the finger or the clitoris, attempting to conceal the inability to know that comes with the peak. In this location, we may find ourselves feeling anxious, frustrated, scrambling, checking out, and perhaps struggling with a sense of disequilibrium.

Erotic practitioners, on the other hand, extend the peak as long as possible, eventually making it a home. The not-knowing becomes the wellspring from which all knowing comes. We recognize that the only self to know is the emergent self, released from the fastening of a stroke to a new variety of potential responses. A source of vibrant discovery rises to the surface.

We may be in the depths of the peak, rich with a dark, aquatic beauty, or we may become breathless in the light, upward strokes of reverence. We may, after nestling in the peak, face the discordant and disruptive stroke of change and extend our state of suspension into what feels like an eternity. We see ourselves revealed in essence. We notice the way our mind is still inclined to wrap itself around the last stroke as a way of avoiding the transition, leaping to a thought or a feeling. Our mind may glide with precision with the finger, and we watch it all at the operating level.

Realizing this is not merely a world in between worlds but a world unto itself, we let it all fall into weightlessness. We feel relief in the continuity. We realize we are never abandoned, only that we abandon the sensation. The terrifying "nothing" is in fact something we can be with.

Change then becomes a beautiful and poignant experience in OM, rather than merely a transition we need to make it through. We enter the liminal, where the old falls away and the new begins to enter. The sensation is of two worlds existing concurrently.

The ultimate gift from this experience is that we are no longer at the mercy of the roller coaster of life. We no longer feel as though we have been dropped from a great height. Because we transition immediately before the sensation is ready to descend, we get to live at the heights of sensation—the most concentrated level of each of the flavors of life.

We inhabit the greatest depth of each of the spots, the most salient forms of the feminine concentration, the heights of reverence, or the richness of the "in-love" spot. We have developed an agile mind that can release exactly when sensation is about to descend, pulling us with it until we take birth inside it. For this reason, we leave when the window opens and enter the weightlessness of the peak. Inhabiting this, we are brought to a new spot that is fresh, alive, and saturated with the next sensation our body hungers for in its ever-deepening intimacy with life.

Peaking in OM

When we enter the peaking stage in OM, Eros courses through the body, bestowing a sensation akin to midair suspension—floating for a moment just after soaring prior to the plunge back down to earth. We become passengers rather than drivers of the experience, and are in the optimal state, able to go in any direction. If we are turned off, we feel disequilibrated, exposed, and flailing.

In this stage, the skills needed for OMing are being able to detect the peak, changing the stroke to maintain resonance, and speaking to stay connected. We practice approval and give ourself over to the stroke.

When stroking someone at the peak, stroking with absolute, crisp precision is important in order to catch the exact moment when the next stroke will have less sensation than the current one. We allow our finger to be moved with buoyancy, an organic levity that is the natural motion in the weightlessness of the peak. Even if the strokee is flailing, we stay steady with our finger and our attention.

When we are being stroked at the peak, tuning in to the sensation of change has us note how the shift in sensation promotes a shift in our mind, and a bridge of awareness builds. If we are turned off in this stage, we may notice fear. We make it the object of our attention and observe the way fear changes its shape. We stay in communication with our partner about what we feel.

56.
THE SIXTH STAGE: EXPRESSION

Expression is the state of flourishing that occurs when we are thriving in the spot of our soul.

Performance is separated from power
Grow your intuition, train your mind
The art of reciprocity is developed
Thriving in the expression of your unique soul

The expression stage has the greatest delineation between its habituated and non-habituated forms. The habituated form is a *display*, which may feel familiar. It is, however, self-conscious rather than erotically conscious—misappropriating Eros and the charge of another person in order to ramp up a sense of power. But it is the opposite of power, because it is disconnected and self-referential. The circuit of power is operating in the mind between our appearance-based ideas.

In the habituated form, the man is often conditioned to focus on the woman's appearance, and the woman on how she is appearing. Insufficient power is flowing from below for our OM partner's attention not to collapse back on itself, or for both of our attention to collapse on each other, rather than landing on and locking into the connection between us. Because of this lack of connection, the Erotic mind falls into the trap of commerce. There is self, and there is other. There is a "doing for," a "being done to," and a "getting for myself."

The circuit is lacking between us that would absorb these distinctions and make the process simply a shared experience. Here, any contact made builds separation rather than dissolves it. A variety of experiences may show up in our OM due to this separation. Actions designed to please our partner become a common occurrence. The thought that we are being used by the other for their respective offering of finger or clitoris takes root. A belief forms that we are entitled to having a certain experience we are not having. Or, maybe we are having it but it feels disconnected. We are using the other to fill a gap in ourselves. A feeling of not deserving forms, and we therefore think we owe the other, so we move to "doing for" energy to pay our perceived debt. We have an impersonal experience of the OM not "doing it" for us. Or we feel like it's too much for us, or is asking too much of us. This occurs when the connection has waned from the physical level of connection.

Any OM not connected at the level of Erotic essence will always present in one of these ways, and will always be the result of lack of power, which can only be accessed from a descent into the body. Because the mind has no real power in itself, it fears the body and must increase its story of separation in order to pump up sensation.

It's vital to note the degraded positions of feeling harmed or of harming, used or using, owed or owing, objectified or objectifying, ungratified or unable to be gratified (or some form abstracted to the impersonal until there is a foundational hopelessness), all invariably result from a lack of Erotic power. This leads to our feedback loop failing to extend to the essence of our partner, remaining locked in our mind.

As the stroker, we start out with an idealistic, seeming virtuosity. In our mind we want to please her, we want to do something for her. We want to offer ourselves to her. We get so much pleasure from her, we can't get enough of her, and we want to devour her. When she does something wonderful to us, we want to turn her on to the degree she turns us on.

In thought or in speech, these are concepts that seem to add to sensation. In reality, they separate and degrade the power of connection and are always limiting, because we are exchanging limited energy—from the limited resource of our mind. If the other person has more energy, our competitive mind feels shamed and has difficulty receiving. If they have less energy, our scarce mind feels robbed. If we have the same energy, both feel depleted by having to spend energy to "get nothing." The end result is always the same: a sense of depletion that, after the initial relief, results in negative thought. This, in turn, is met with an attempt to get more, an aversion to that type of experience, or ignoring the feeling. What we would otherwise call connection can now scarcely be called contact.

In this phase we have narrowed our options down: the one thing that will bring gratification is the offering of ourselves to the Eros that lies between us and our partner. True connection can only occur inside the shared space of Eros, where the single question that exists is, how do we turn the lights on and experience that which can only happen when essence meets essence?

Both partners focus on their part in this endeavor, finding the reward in the doing. As strokers, we have an opportunity to train the mind to play the instrument of the body and hear its music. As strokees, we learn how to be played, where to hold the energy, where to open, and how to transmit the radiation of Eros.

Gratification comes internally, through learning the art of reciprocity and attuned feedback; the learning occurs as a reward in itself—the music of light both partners get to exist within.

This presence, the state of pure Eros resulting from the open-loop circuitry of two nervous systems locked in connection, is the holistic experience we are all seeking—the experience is of two human beings, each vertically connected, above in the ideal and below in power. The cycle is complete with enlightenment from above, mysticism from below, and humanity and heart in between; none of the three alone will gratify us—only the three in unison can.

With the three together, we find ourselves in *eudaimonia*, the state of human flourishing, occurring when we are thriving in our *funktionslust* as human beings, when we are doing what we are here to do. We find ourselves in a virtuous cycle: we receive more power, and in receiving more power we are able to connect more deeply with our purpose. In other words, living in our function, the "spot" of our soul, not only brings about a deep-seated sense of flourishing and unimaginable gratification, it also equips us to go more deeply into the spot to naturally and organically generate more of the same.

The key is a simple shift in focus, and this shift impacts everything. Instead of focusing on ourselves or the other, we focus on the connection in between us. We always respond there first. The sensation and lighting there will never lie; it will always instruct. The connection will not betray or deceive us. In the connection is a voice that arises and guides our response. Some call this voice intuition. We find we are often unwilling to do anything for a finite being, but that we are willing to do anything for the infinite source that lies between us. As a result, we realize our potential and become who we wish to be.

Expression in OM

The stage of expression in OM is marked by a lot of external expressions of Eros, ranging from flushing to contractions, from swelling to ejaculation. Uncontrollable sounds may be emitted, along with shuddering and shaking. We take great care, however, not to get lost in the appearance. If we are turned on, our emanation of expression is in equal proportion to what we are receiving and we feel aligned with Eros. If we are turned off in this stage, we have a sense of fearful incompetence. Our sense of power may be an overblown sense or we may feel like a fraud and fear being found out.

The ability to turn our stroker on from the strokee position is a skill that is relevant in the expression stage. Here, we also learn to allow Eros to fill the room. We avoid under-extension and over-extension.

When stroking someone in expression, we stroke to run the energy, using intention to add to whichever direction exhibits great intensity. An increase in feelings of desire, love, and lust may rise to the surface at this level but we don't personalize them. Noticing where vocalizations increase or where body tension increases and the underlying sensation decreases has us peak early. We ensure the stroking matches the underlying sensation. If we are turned off, we may find ourselves focusing on appearance rather than connection, requiring us to continue to draw the attention back to connection. We take nothing personally, including the expression of delight or anger. Sexual thoughts may increase, threatening to pull us into focusing on our partner; however, avoiding this is important, as is maintaining focus on the sensation, without gripping to it as it moves through us.

As the strokee in expression, "letting it out" has us enjoy the expression. We OM in search of sensation, not effect. Frequent OMing helps us extend our capacity to be in high-intensity states without going over. If we are turned off, stiffening or hardening our body may be tempting but has the potential to evoke a demanding sensation. Volition is introduced here so we deliberately surrender at this time. We make requests as the power goes up because the stroker may need the addition of voice. The essence of sexuality may enter, but we resist the temptation to parlay it into anything other than sensation.

57.
THE SEVENTH STAGE: PLAY

The outward expression of something beyond, drawn in and down. The sensation conferred is one of being touched and used by the divine.

What is static is made dynamic
Consciousness channels power
Has humor and resourcefulness
The full, unimpeded, natural expression of yourself emerges

Once the foundation of connection is set and the inherent laws of classical OM are learned, practiced, and brought down to the bones, a new level of OM is birthed. Our system of connection is secure enough that a new level of Eros is able to flow through, carrying with it a sense of improvisation, genius, and intuition that subsumes the technical. Eros then begins to lift off from the solid base where we have learned to remain connected to power, regardless of what threatens to call us back to the tumescent mind. OM now ventures into play consciousness.

Often seen as a consciousness lacking skill, play consciousness is the channel that requires the greatest mastery. We must know the classical rules in order to play with them well. To play with rules well is to be elevated into a state of transcendent brilliance, where there is a sense of divinity pouring forth—an incandescence. In the suspension of this moment, the body and mind are channels of a presence that permeates all. This presence is the expression of something beyond, drawn in and down, and expressed outwardly, so the sensation conferred is one of having been touched and used by the divine.

But when we play with the rules poorly, we activate our tumescent mind. With this level of power pouring through, the activation occurs not only as an invasive force, it becomes trapped energy in the body. Not only do we feel unskilled, we may feel overburdened and useless. The nature of the play channel is high risk and high return. The reward is the thrill of discovery, seeing what we are made of, and testing our resilience and creativity.

If this stage posed a question, it would be: "What is possible?" This is this channel where we tap into the infinite nature of OM, the vast and endless doorways of sensory perception that can be opened to worlds nested within worlds.

This channel is the agency or expressive side of the activation of life. The experience of life force, activated in turn-on, comes into contact with OM in this stage. We feel a profound wonder, curiosity, and a desire to discover. These are not states that can be manufactured, and they are not the results of reactions; they are a reflection of our internal sentience extending further into the world, led by our curiosity.

This state sits upon the fundamentals. Eros has drawn the mind down into the body, creating a reaction that releases power. This released power produces an initial expression that must be grounded and mastered. Only then are we ready to elevate the rules we play by from the standard to the intuitive. To be clear, we are still playing within a set of rules. We all have an unalterable, innate sense of the elegant harmony of sensations, and we are allowing our intuitive sense to guide us.

What we once perceived as obstacles become opportunities that we convert into skills. Sensations that were previously too high to meet, spots that were closed, and speeds that seemed too fast, all become the playground of exploration.

Play through Reception

The primary reason the play stage is seen as a type of mastery is that it stems from a security of connection, allowing both partners to lock into a state of yes. In this state, we have the capacity to open to any stroke or sensation and we trust that our partner does as well. This trust enables us to take risks. We may assume the person receiving is the most vulnerable; in reality, it is the person stroking. The stroker is at the mercy of the person being stroked.

As strokees, we hold the power to make the stroker either great or a flop by drawing out either greatness or ineptitude. This is where things get interesting, where the world gets set right side up, where we discover, in practice rather than theory, that the person receiving is the one who has the most potential to determine the direction of the OM. The key to making a stroker into a genius is what we call *brilliant reception*.

Brilliant reception is created when the strokee activates enough power to awaken the force of genius. We do this by applying the attention of approval on the sensation of power—the reaction within is genius. From here we draw from the genius within, which is of course Eros, through the stroker's finger. In essence, we are stroking with our *reception*, and we are able to extract genius from the stroker in proportion to the activation of our own genius. We possess the ability to draw forth any sensation from the stroke—from love to illumination to relaxation—to the level that these characteristics have been activated in ourselves. We hold the capacity to clear any blockages within the stroker, absorb congested energy, convert it using the heat of Eros in us, and send it back as pure Eros.

When we say "yes" to the stroke we are giving and to the stroke we are receiving, we are ready to explore all spots, speeds, directions, and variations. We listen closely to Eros, to the music, as we engage in this.

The strokee's power is in her reception, in her yes. Our world and our experience of it is created through this yes. Our yes is rooted in our agreement to approve of whatever we receive, because approval means opening to, and anything opened to is experienced as pleasurable. Something may be sad, beautiful, or even painful, but there can be a pleasure to each of these. We are agreeing not to get lost in the single dimension of the sensation, but to focus on the flow of the process through our body. In other words, by remaining open, any sensation has a pleasurable element and tone, whether it's somber, alive, or angry.

To the extent we are able to keep the tone flowing with the music of pleasure, it continues to move and change, enabling it to be received fully in the body. Preventing our mind from listening only to the individual note, extracting it, and then focusing on it in the isolation of the mind is key; doing so confines us to living in the story of the sensation.

Play only exists in an in-the-moment, improvisational flow, when we have the capacity to meet whatever enters. This is what brings about the sensation of delight, which is the marker of the stage of play.

Play for Freedom

In the play channel, delight is found in the catch and toss of the full expression between the ever-resilient and resourceful Erotic bodies of each partner. This dynamic cannot occur if one or the other cannot maintain a play consciousness, where the foundational agreement is to say "yes."

Because we are permitted to fully let ourselves out without fear of harming the other, play is the place where we see what we are made of. We can do this because our partner agrees they are a co-creator and cannot be harmed because they are choosing to be open to all experiences.

Until we have this agreement, our souls cannot meet. This phenomenon cannot be partial; we cannot hold part of ourselves back and meet another's soul. Such a meeting only happens when two souls are 100 percent activated and 100 percent available. The tumescent mind can, and will, make the process sound complicated, but it's not; it is quite simple, which doesn't mean it's not difficult. It happens when we agree to say "yes" to our experiences. What we discover is that this is the only way to activate the Erotic mind, the mind that knows.

Inside each of us is an eternally resilient mind that knows how to open, absorb, and convert every single experience into love, then send it back out as love. The finger that switches this mind on is the word yes.

Yes to our fight, yes to our resistance, yes to our hurt, and yes to our feeling of wrongdoing. Eventually, we confront the most terrifying yes of all, what all play is practice for: yes to the full, unimpeded, natural expression of ourselves. When we hit this yes, we hit the yes of genius. This expression is something we can never figure out because it comes as an outgrowth. It liberates itself in an instant and reveals itself wholly. Suddenly, we know.

The old rules of play are pretty basic: we play to win, using the rules to move us closer to winning and further from not winning, which is perceived as losing. Discrimination and the capacity to say "no" is vital. When one or both players win, the game is over. Connection is secondary to winning, and personal expression takes a back seat to the goal. From the perspective of Eros, this type of winning is merely climaxing or having our conditioning met—maybe falling in love, getting married, or acquiring some sign of commitment.

The new rules, on the other hand, are to play in order to keep playing, to play to discover what is possible, and to do this by playing *with* the rules. We play with the rules in order to activate a genuine, spontaneous novelty that activates attention and adds to its complexity. And all of this is done to learn the mechanics of unique expression while in connection; both partners agree to fully contribute their unique expression to the connection and to draw from it as well, playing off each other.

This is the location of freedom. But this is not freedom *from*, which doesn't exist. Freedom from is just well-dressed separation. This is freedom *with*, where we play all-out, exactly as we are, not in spite of but for the benefit of all. We do this by focusing on what lies between us.

Play in OM

When we are in the play stage in OM, we feel more powerful below the surface. Our body feels entirely effortless and even volatile, with a feeling of continuous current flowing at the point of contact, and the easeful following of Eros. Any direction we go in is good at this stage where we are in flow. Our body feels volatile, involuntary, and pliant, and the boundary of our physical body feels fluid. We have the sense we are more felt than heard. We enter a timelessness and are completely absorbed as our body disappears into Eros. If we are turned off in this stage, we have a sense of superiority and are distant and mistrusting. We find ourselves willfully efforting.

The skills we need in the play stage are humor, resourcefulness, risk-taking, and resiliency in the face of resistance.

When we are stroking someone in play, sensation is magnified, with the stroke felt at the level of attention. Strokes are more energetic than physical. If our partner is turned off, we stroke with precision at the highest point of sensation rather than stroking harder and faster. Our attention may be drawn to every thought; here, we remember our rightness and our partner's rightness unwaveringly. Stroking to nuzzle the gates of the spot open and then dancing in the current, we pour our own Erotic body through our finger.

When we are being stroked in play, we activate our Erotic body and draw in all strokes from the stroker. Our clitoris plays back and we use our attention to foster the natural unfolding. If we find we are turned off, we notice any blocking and continue to bring ourselves to *the third* that exists between us and our partner.

58.

THE EIGHTH STAGE: STILLNESS

The mind has been subsumed into the body, and Erotic vision opens.

> An absence of activity and distraction
> Letting go of preference
> Moving to resilience rather than sensitivity
> The elegance of Eros is revealed

Stillness, from the habituated mind, is an escape from activity, used as a weapon, a means of withdrawing or retreating from life. In Eros, on the other hand, we sink into stillness as a way to deepen our relationship with life and allow the delight of activity, of the challenging and the transcendent, to assimilate in our body. Stillness is like an enzyme that metabolizes experience and reveals yet deeper truth.

The habituated version of stillness is an absence; in Eros, stillness is a location that is anything but absent. Stillness in Eros is filled with a silence that is palpable to the Erotic senses. It is always here, in the in-between, our mind subsumed by our body. From this merging we emerge into stillness. Mind and body operate in unison to open the dimension of stillness. Inside this dimension, space exists for a specific aspect of Erotic vision to open.

As strokers, we may not even be stroking the clitoris, only the lube. We sense that our breath would almost be distracting, and so breathing occurs through the skin with a feeling of suspension to the experience, as though consciousness has been extracted and isolated from the laws of the manifest aspects of OM. The maelstrom of dynamic energy is brought to an altogether different vision: a location of unchanging reality upon which the drama of the OM cycle plays itself out.

Our mind, having made its descent and being tapped into power, is now a different mind from before. Whereas previously there might have been a stream of thought that merely "took" the mind, the mind now has the power to hold itself out of this stream of thought, aiming the spotlight of attention solely on the stillness at the point of connection. It is able to maintain attention there, and when sustained, this simple placement of attention releases tremendous sensations, from goose bumps to what feels like tiny jolts of electricity, waves, and even involuntary rocking that moves through the whole of our body. Here, Eros reveals the hidden truth of elegance.

From seeming inactivity, what is offered is a potential for massive response. We allow our mind to simply notice the expressions of the body and bathe in the pleasure. The pleasure feels akin to what we might consider arousing, given the excitement of it, as if it were carbonated. The law of conservation of nature reveals itself, as does the aliveness of space. We do nothing. We remain here and are "done to."

In the stillness, another door may open, a sinking in as if the body has released the excitement and can drop into another layer, one that exudes a maturity. A full and weighted quality carries with it a calming serenity that does not create, but reveals peace.

Since there is nothing to "get," our mind doesn't chase this peace, but sinks in even further. It *allows*. It's as if the mind sinks through a layer of itself into something deep and comforting. The comfort has always been there. Our mind, in its activity, had been caught in the various traps of stuffed and starving, tired and wired, all-knowing and useless, rejecting and regretful; now it spreads out to contain all of the above, without ever getting caught on one side.

In this place, our mind can unfurl even further into our body. A beautiful sense of optionality opens—pure potential. Being is equal and simultaneous in all directions, while at the same time it's as if the mind has returned to its home with no need to go anywhere.

By way of warning: the two states we are most likely to become addicted to are restoration—entailing pleasure and homeostasis—and stillness. Each is a home setting; the former is the home of our separate body, and the latter is the home of our separate mind. When the stroke comes that would have us move from this location, we might feel a tug—the temptation to refuse to leave.

Without the power of our body, this channel of stillness can also bring with it a dilettante quality of demand. Over-sensitization is common for people stuck on this channel; they have become addicted to depth as an escape rather than as a celebration, using it to fill a perceived emptiness rather than as a beautiful location to experience.

If our mind lacks power, it may not enter other locations well. At the same time, because the drive of the mind is to know, our mind may not admit this, instead exalting this location above all others. If this happens, we do not buy into it.

All stages have equal and endless potential for discovery and mastery. Some of us may spend a whole lifetime mastering one stage. But the work of OM is to develop equal and simultaneous facility in all stages, as they are the channels that carry the sensation of life. We build this capacity so when the channel changes, the aspect of mind related to the new channel is there to meet it, at least in potential. In an OM, when the stroke comes, we are there to meet it fully.

We meet life on life's terms and, in return, life gives us intimacy with life.

Stillness in OM

When we are in stillness in OM, we feel free from time and space with our body as an open channel. Both the stroker and strokee feel in union as one, experiencing the same thing. We remember there is no wrong way to OM—everything is right and good. There is connection regardless of the stroke, as both people are fully surrendered. We open to space beyond our physical body.

Aiming attention to the point of connection and sustaining it allows the mind to drop and focus on feeling the pleasure. Then, focusing on the calm, we allow it to drop again. It will land in optionality and naturally unfold. What feels like deeper truths may reveal themselves. We listen but do not grasp, moving when the stroke changes. If we are turned off, our mind is fussy, demanding, hypersensitive, and irritated. If we find stillness, we focus on this stillness, continuing to aim our attention inside of ourselves. If there is not stillness, we allow ourselves to be moved without gripping to the location. Turned-off stillness is often a refusal to come up from the depths.

THE CONTAINER AND FORM OF ORGASMIC MEDITATION

Orgasmic Meditation takes place within a set of standardized, mutually agreed-upon parameters we refer to as *the container*. You've probably experienced a container before while playing a game. Games often have nonnegotiable rules like you can't use your hands in soccer or you can only move certain pieces on the chessboard in a particular way. Break the fundamental defining characteristics of the game and you're not playing the game anymore. The OM container features corresponding elements.

The distinctions contained in this section are crucial to understanding that OM is a specific practice performed under detailed instructions and compliance guidelines. OM relies on container consistency and the knowledge that at no time will there be a request to change the container.

When we refer to OM, we are making direct reference to the elements of the container and form that follows.

The Institute of OM (instituteofom.com) maintains an expanded, comprehensive, and periodically revised version of OM training resources.

In OM, the function of the container is to relax our *vigilance*. Vigilance is the faculty of mind that kicks in to make sure we're safe in cases where we feel our safety may be threatened. For example, vigilance is responsible for that extra-sensitive awareness we feel when walking down a quiet street at night and times when we sense that somebody has an ulterior motive. Vigilance is characterized scientifically as being related to the learned avoidance of pain and refers to the functions of our minds that are ready to protect us from actual or potential threats. Because so many of our negative past experiences are associated with interpersonal relationships and the feelings of disappointment, hurt, confusion, and powerlessness that seem to come with them, it makes sense that vigilance would rise up to protect us in the face of a physically connected experience involving genital contact like OM. Vigilance is like a loyal guard dog—we want its protection under the right circumstances yet we don't want it snarling at everybody and everything. How can we retrain this part of ourselves?

The container demonstrates to vigilance that the potential dangers that occupy it have already been mitigated, thereby relieving it of its duties. Quite literally, it is meant to *contain* us safely so our vigilance does not have to. Over time, the repetition of OMing within the container builds a sense of consistency and predictability. As a result, our vigilance relaxes to greater and greater degrees, allowing us more and more contact with the parts of ourselves vigilance had previously obscured. As we learn to rely on the container for solidity, we naturally begin to loosen up. Each aspect of the container is unchanging and non-negotiable, further adding to its dependability.

The procedural aspects of OM exist to offer us a set of standardized conditions that facilitate Erotic exchange. However, the container of OM, while important, would be an empty set of gestures without that which comes through it.

By creating a nest and holding the container, we enter into partnership with Eros, who without those things would remain unwed as diffuse potential. By being willing to release our grip on the agenda of achievement, we communicate to Eros that our love is unconditional—that she may manifest in whatever form she prefers and by carving out a time just for our communion that we will remain with her as she unfolds. Having the experience for its own sake conveys that we know we are better for having been in her presence, that to demand anything more would equate to being paid double. She is the honored guest in this oasis set against the backdrop of dehydrating, endless activity. We honor her by observing her customs and showing her this hospitality. And it is then that Eros feels safe enough to enter.

As it is the visible, technical, procedural element of the practice, learning the various procedural steps and forms immediately, ironically, becomes easy bait for the protective aspect of the rational mind that seeks to demonstrate competence. This is ironic as this aspect of mind is the first thing the container is meant to calm; it is this aspect of mind that is relentlessly searching for a formula and a "right way." As such, the rational mind often can't see the forest for the trees. The rational mind will surely take some time focusing earnestly on these elements of the container as it learns to trust and function within it, eventually coming to its first hard-won summit: conscious competence. Here, the rational mind can flex in its proficiency as it has and knows its duty, and can focus on it throughout the experience.

The rational mind, now posted in its rightful place as attendant, watches awestruck as Eros is finally able to enter and saturate. In the reality of the container, there is a correct form and an incorrect form. Once inside and holding the container, Eros, as she is prone to do, deepens the game. We realize with Eros, not only can we not "do it wrong," but relaxing the mind that is trying to "do it right" is the philosopher's stone of the experience. As we cross into the stillness of hallowed time and in the sanctitude of hallowed space, we feel the shift, that the environment is safe enough, and now is the time to turn our attention toward our inner life. We realize it is not only Eros who needs the container, it is also us.

Consent

Consent in OM is a continuous process that begins when you say yes to an OM and continues upon entry into the nest and, provided both partners follow the protocols, is affirmed by each partner's words and actions until the OM is complete. This means that all steps, including those that involve physical contact, imply consent unless either partner, at any moment, verbally withdraws their consent. In this case, the OM stops immediately.

This might be a challenging aspect of the practice for some. OM can be considered an environment for practicing being present, engaged, and communicative while actively giving consent to another person. Both partners need to navigate their own sense of safety and communicate about their internal state during an OM. Again, OM provides a setting for this exploration.

This process can involve opting out of the experience at any time. In OM, you practice stating what you need and want, including if you need to stop an OM. It's crucial that both partners are responsible, empowered, and care about their own experience enough that either would stop the OM at any time if asked. Should you find yourself in a situation where you want to stop the OM, you are responsible for verbally informing your partner. This could be as simple as announcing, "I want to stop the OM now." A response can be as simple as, "Thank you," "Okay," or "Yes." At this point both people should stop what they are doing and exit the nest.

The Container and Form of Orgasmic Meditation

PRIMARY ASPECTS OF THE CONTAINER

- The steps of OM must be followed in order and without omission or modification
- Fifteen-minute timed stroking period
- Stroker remains fully clothed while the strokee only removes the necessary clothing to expose the genitals
- Stroker must use gloves, regardless of the nature of the OM partner's existing relationship

THE FORM OF ORGASMIC MEDITATION

In this section, we're going to lay out the steps of OM. Within each step we find techniques, protocols, and sequences for completing certain aspects of the practice. These steps include directions like stroke only using up or down motions as opposed to side-to-side motions, place your hands on your partner's thighs with your fingers together, not apart, and make requests by asking for something specific about the stroke to change. These descriptions are aspects of *form*. If the container is like the rules of a game, the form is how you play it. They tell us how to do what we do inside the container.

Form exists on a continuum from poor form to good form. There is a reason behind everything you're told to do within the OM container. Poor form will typically lead to poor results. Good form will typically lead to good results. Some aspects of form can be customized while others are simply meant to be followed without deviation. What follows are explanations of what the form of each step looks like and how you can customize these forms for your particular body or situation.

Step 1: Ask for an OM

The first step in OM is one person asking another person to OM. Both people must be trained in the practice of OM. If the person receiving the request doesn't know what they're saying "yes" to, it's not an OM.

In OM, we ask in a way that reflects the notion that both partners are doing something together—not that one partner is doing something to or for the other. So we say something like, "Would you like to have an OM?" as opposed to, "Can I OM you?" Do you hear the difference?

The person receiving the request to OM is free to accept or decline with or without explanation. People say "no" for many reasons that aren't personal. If you get a "no," simply say, "Thank you," and remember it might just be no for right now. Unless otherwise requested, you always have the option to ask again another time.

When asking somebody to OM, keep the request simple and separate. This means we don't mix invitations to OM with other invitations, such as, "Would you like to OM *and* take a walk?" When we combine invitations, it might bring up feelings of obligation to do both when we only want to do one of them. By keeping invitations separate you know what you are saying "yes" to, and what you are saying "no" to. This keeps OMing partnerships clear and clean.

One of the features of OM is that it is based in simplicity in that at each stage we do and use nothing more or less than what's needed. In keeping with this principle, OM doesn't rely on any other activities or kinds of relationships between practice partners. This way, when somebody asks you to OM, you can be sure that's all they're asking.

Here are a few examples of correct and incorrect form for asking and responding to requests to OM.

CORRECT FORM FOR ASKING SOMEBODY TO OM:

"Would you like to have an OM?" "Would you like to OM?"

INCORRECT FORM:

"Will you stroke me?" "Can I OM you?"
"We should OM sometime!"

Can you hear the difference?

CORRECT FORM TO RESPOND TO AN OFFER TO OM:

"Yes, I would like to OM."
"No, I would not like to OM."
"No, thanks."
"Love to, sounds great."

INCORRECT FORM TO RESPOND TO AN OFFER TO OM:

"I guess so."
"I'm not comfortable yet, but let's do it anyway."
"Maybe," or "Maybe later."

If you've agreed to OM, set a date, time, and location. If you're OMing right now, you can begin to set up the nest.

Sometimes partners make an agreement to have a regularly scheduled OM at a particular date, time, and location. In this case, you do not have to ask every time. You can always change such an agreement at any time, for any reason.

Step 2: Set Up the Nest

First, a well-lit space is essential. Make sure you set up your nest in a location where you can see clearly.

Now, regarding the supplies, you may already have some of these items and others you may need to acquire:

- *Yoga mat.* It is suggested that practitioners OM in a neutral location like a floor as opposed to a bed. If your floor is hard, a yoga mat can add increased comfort for the strokee. It's optional but recommended.

- *A blanket for the strokee to lie down on.* Any blanket folded into a long rectangle will work. This provides a soft, comfortable place to lie down and goes on top of the yoga mat if you're using one.

- *At least three pillows.* It's important for both partners to be comfortable and physically supported during the practice. Three pillows is a good amount to start with, and you may need more depending on the shape of your body and how it meshes with your partner's body.

- *A meditation cushion or something firm for the stroker to sit on.* If a cushion isn't available, a stack of blankets can be substituted. It's important for the stroker to have a firm seating cushion of adequate height.

- *Washcloths.* We recommend buying a new set of small washcloths to be used strictly for OM. The washcloth is used to collect excess lubricant in the concluding steps of the OM. Use a clean washcloth each time you OM.

- *Lubricant.* For OM, you will need lubricant. We have tested many kinds and recommend using an oil-based lubricant that maintains viscosity rather than thin silicon or water-based lubricants as they tend to dry out or otherwise dissipate easily.

- *Timer.* You will need a timer to precisely measure fifteen minutes with an interval bell at the thirteen-minute mark.

- *Well-fitting gloves for the stroker.* Gloves are part of the practice and serve multiple purposes. The first is that they offer a protective barrier. Remember when we talked about vigilance earlier on? The gloves remove the question about whether the stroker washed their hands or how thoroughly they washed them. Even one tiny bit of bacteria under a fingernail can cause issues. Gloves remove any doubt and allow the mind to relax. The second purpose for gloves is that for OM partners who might be physically intimate in other ways, the gloves provide a clear signal that OM belongs solely in its own context.

The way you set up the supplies for an OM is always the same, and the way you set up those supplies matters. Take your time, and deliberately place everything where it belongs.

WHERE SHOULD WE PLACE THE NEST?

Set up your nest in a space that feels relaxing to you. Most practitioners find a location on the floor of a room in their living space. As we've mentioned, if you can avoid using a bed, we strongly suggest doing so. Make sure your space is comfortable, well lit, and secure.

Now it's time to arrange the nest. Here's how you do it:

- Lay out the yoga mat and place the blanket on top of it. Make sure both are straight and smooth.

- Next, place a pillow at the top for the strokee's head.

- Place two more pillows at both sides of the blanket midway down for support under the strokee's left knee and the stroker's right knee.

- Place the washcloth next to the firm cushion in the middle of the blanket directly under where the strokee's genitals will be.

- Place the gloves, lubricant, and timer in a location that is within reach for the stroker once seated in the nest, usually just to their right.

- Next, prepare the timer so that when it's time to start the fifteen-minute countdown, it's ready to go.

- Now, both stroker and strokee are ready to get into position.

Step 3: Getting into Position

Now that you've set up the nest, the next step is getting into it. Getting into the OM position can be a little awkward to start with but learning what feels comfortable for you and your partner physically and becoming comfortable with the practice overall tend to go hand in hand.

STROKEE

First, undress from the waist down. Then, lie down in the nest with your head resting on the pillow. Make sure the washcloth is centered under your genital area. With your knees raised, place your feet on the ground and let your left knee fall open onto the left pillow. Your right knee will eventually rest on your stroker's leg, so it can simply stay put. Find a position for your arms that feels comfortable. It's common to extend your arms out, or by your sides, or rest them on your torso. Stay relaxed and remember to breathe normally.

STROKER

Position the meditation cushion against your partner's right hip. Standing behind the cushion, place your right foot to the right of the cushion. Then take your left foot and step over your partner's body, placing that foot near their left hip.

Slowly lower yourself to sit on the cushion. The sole of your left foot should be flat on the ground, and your left leg extends over your partner's waist, knee bent in the air. Be careful to not rest the weight of the left leg on her stomach.

Your right leg will naturally slide out to the side at a comfortable angle, bending slightly at the knee so the sole of your right foot faces away from you. Your right knee rests on the right pillow.

STROKEE

Strokee, once your partner is seated comfortably, bring your right leg over the stroker's right leg. Communicate with the stroker to adjust the pillow arrangement so your right leg feels adequately supported. You can ask for additional pillows if needed.

This is a good time for the stroker to notice their body position. You are aiming to have your left knee at approximately the midpoint over the strokee's body, so the top of your knee is more or less over the strokee's belly button. Now, rest your left elbow directly on the left kneecap. Notice when you swivel your arm down, does your hand land directly over your strokee's genitals? This is the orientation we're aiming for. There should be little to no tension in the left shoulder.

Note: this is also a good time to notice if you are comfortable. Do either of you feel like you need more pillows or does the stroker need to sit up a little higher? Feel free to experiment with multiple additional pillows and supports. Fifteen minutes can become a very long time without the proper comfort.

GETTING OUT OF POSITION

To get out of the position at the end of an OM, the stroker swivels their left leg toward the right side of the nest, and the strokee swivels her right leg toward the left side of the nest. The stroker can then offer to help the strokee up to a seated position.

Step 4. Safeporting

Now we're going to take you through the series of steps leading up to the point where the stroking section of the OM begins.

In Step 4, we begin by introducing you to a new term known as *safeporting*. Safeporting is when one person tells another what they're going to do before they do it. The benefit of safeporting is that knowing what to expect before it occurs has us relax and feel prepared. We safeport people all the time when we tell them things like we're turning the heat off in the house or leaving to take the dog for a walk. Implicit in these safeports is a preemptive "reason why": a reason why the house may get cold; a reason why we can't find the dog. Safeporting removes ambiguity and surprise and is especially helpful if we're already feeling vigilant. A doctor might safeport you before touching you or doing something that might cause discomfort or surprise. A distinction here is that safeporting isn't asking permission. It's doing somebody the kindness of letting them know what's going to happen and when. Safeporting occurs here in this step and again in a few minutes when genital contact is made for the first time.

For the first safeport, the stroker will announce that they will be placing their hands on the thighs of the strokee.

The form of this communication should be simple and basic. The stroker can say, "I'm going to touch your thighs now," or, "I'm going to give you some grounding pressure now." Once the stroker has given this safeport, Step 4 is complete.

The strokee can respond with a simple acknowledgment like "Okay," or, "Thank you."

Step 5. Grounding Pressure Is Applied

At this point, the stroker places their hands on the strokee's thighs—right hand on the inner right thigh, and left hand on the inner left thigh—with slightly more pressure than they would use were they just resting them there. The hands are placed midway between the knee and hips with medium pressure, fingers close together. The hands remain still and in position for about ten seconds. This is a great moment for both partners to take a deep breath, sink in, and place their attention on what they feel in their own bodies. Once the stroker's hands have been in place for a few moments, you've completed Step 5.

The purpose of this step is to establish a basic physical connection that both partners can relax into known as *grounding*. Knowing you're going to have an OM can stir up unexpected feelings and sensations. Grounding brings our attention to the body through the physical contact it offers and smooths that feeling out without losing its energizing quality.

The stroker keeps their hands on the strokee's thighs while they continue into the next step, noticing.

Step 6: Noticing

The noticing step is where the stroker looks at their partner's genitals and describes some physical characteristics of what they see in a *value-neutral* manner. Value neutral simply means described in terms of color, shape, texture, or size without adding positive or negative connotations also known as *value judgments*.

So for instance, the stroker may say something like, "I notice a light-pink color on the outside of your left outer labia," or, "There is a small, dark dot on the skin of your clitoral hood."

Here the strokee can simply say, "Thank you," to acknowledge the communication.

An example of what not to say would be offering a metaphor or value-laden adjectives like, "Your inner labia look like a rose," or, "Your introitus is so beautiful." Keep it simple. No need to get fancy.

The purpose of this step is to anchor both partners' attention on the strokee's genitals, and it's an opportunity for both partners to become present. For the stroker, notice if you find yourself wanting to add value judgments on top of the simple description. You can just notice that and let it go.

For many strokees, being noticed in this way is a new experience and it may be helpful to journal about it afterward.

Once you've completed the noticing step, you're done with Step 6.

Step 7: Put on Gloves

At this point, you're in the nest. You've completed one safeport, you've grounded, and you've completed the noticing step. Now, it's time for the stroker to put on gloves.

Best glove practices for the stroker:

- When you go to put on the gloves, try to keep the right elbow or forearm connected to the strokee's thigh to maintain the physical connection you established during grounding.

- You'll also want to make sure the glove is flat and as free from wrinkles as possible against the pad of your left index finger.

- It's a good idea to have an extra glove around and ready in case a glove tears.

- Having some baby powder around in case your hands are sweaty helps to put the glove on smoothly. Try to avoid getting baby powder on the outside of your glove.

- Remember, gloves are part of the practice and must be worn no matter what.

Step 8: Apply Lubricant

Next, the stroker applies a nickel-sized amount of lubricant to their left index finger and lightly coats the pad of the right thumb.

Step 9: The Second Safeport

We've already introduced the word "safeport." The stroker is going to use it again now in Step 9 to begin the sequence of steps that leads us into the stroking portion of the OM.

Step 9 is the second safeport. The stroker will say, "I'm going to touch your genitals now," to let the strokee know genital contact is about to occur. As with the first safeport, the strokee can simply acknowledge with "Thank you," or, "Okay."

Step 10: Start the Timer

Step 10 occurs directly afterward. In Step 10, the stroker starts the fifteen-minute timer commencing the stroking portion of the OM.

Step 11: The Stroking Portion

The stroking portion of the OM begins with the lube stroke—the first moment of genital contact. The lube stroke has two forms, which follow these sequences, respectively.

FORM A:

1. Using the left thumb and middle finger, gently part the strokee's outer labia. Drop the tip of the left index finger to the base of the introitus while keeping the labia parted with the middle finger and thumb—and slowly move the left index fingertip up from the base of the introitus, up through the parted labia, to the clitoris.
2. Allow the left middle finger to break contact while the left thumb slides to the top of the clitoral hood. The thumb rests just above the hood, pulling it back to expose the glans of the clitoris.
3. Once the left index finger and thumb are situated, the right thumb is placed at the base of the introitus, simply resting stationary with no more than a centimeter or two of the thumbnail over the threshold of the introitus while applying light pressure downward. The rest of the right hand can rest on the ground or be placed under the strokee's bottom, knuckles down. Strokers can simply say, "Lift up," at this point, and the strokee lifts her hips up slightly, the stroker's right hand slides under, and the strokee can then let her hips return to the ground, now resting on the underside of the stroker's right fingers.

That is lube stroke form A. Alternately, if the strokee's anatomy does not permit the easeful use of this form, a second form of the lube stroke can be used—form B.

FORM B:

1. Using the middle and ring fingers of each hand, gently part the outer labia on either side—left fingers on left labia and right fingers on right labia—and with the tip of the left index finger, slowly move it up from the base of the introitus between the parted labia to the clitoris.

2. The left thumb is placed at the top of the clitoral hood and the fingers that were parting the labia are released. The thumb rests just above the hood, pulling it back to expose more of the clitoris.
3. Once the left index finger and thumb are situated, the right thumb is placed at the base of the introitus, simply resting stationary with no more than a centimeter or two of the thumbnail over the threshold of the introitus while applying light pressure downward. The rest of the right hand can rest on the ground or be placed under the strokee's bottom. Strokers can simply say, "Lift up," at this point, and the strokee lifts her hips up slightly, the stroker's right hand slides under, and the strokee can then let her hips return to the ground, now resting on the underside of the stroker's right fingers.

A COUPLE OF NOTES:

- The execution of the lube stroke is a key moment as it's when the clitoris is located and touched for the first time. The two forms of lube stroke offer a pair of practical options to best meet different anatomical (both genital and body shape/size/flexibility) combinations. Test it out for yourself and pick the one that works best.

- From time to time, relative physical size and flexibility issues may prevent strokers from placing the right thumb at the base of the introitus. In such cases, the right hand may be placed on the strokee's right thigh or placed somewhere else out of the way.

- The left middle, ring, and pinkie fingers can also remain in stationary contact with the left labia as a means of stabilizing the left hand if desired.

- It's helpful to keep the left thumb free from lubricant or other moisture. Its job is to hold the hood of the clitoris open so it relies on a certain degree of friction. If it's slippery, it won't be able to do that. That said, sometimes the left thumb gets lube on it, and you cannot do anything about it. The left fingertip can still sense the location of the clitoris and stroke. Though it will feel a bit different, there is no reason to stop the OM and clean off the thumb; if you want to, you can, but it's not necessary

Now we're going to break down the hand position you'll be using to stroke with.

First, hold up your left hand in a C shape. Turn that C shape downward toward the ground so it becomes an upside-down U. Next, ball up each finger except the index and thumb. Last, slightly hook the end of your index finger. That's your stroking hand. This is what your hand will look like after the end of the lube stroke.

You're now in position for the stroking portion of the OM.

We will discuss more about the strokes in later sections. For now, know that strokes only occur in upward or downward direction, never side to side.

COMMUNICATION DURING AN OM

As the stroking portion of the OM proceeds, sometimes one partner may have an intuitive sense of how the dimensions of the current stroke might be adjusted to produce greater resonance, like more pressure or perhaps less speed. OM includes a protocol to facilitate this type of communication in the form of offers from the stroker and requests from the strokee.

Offers and requests introduce an opportunity for collaborative experimentation between partners. Neither partner has to be positive that their adjustment will be "right." Getting it "right" is not, after all, the point: letting sensation guide the experience is. Because strokes are already measured in terms of pressure, speed, length, direction, and location, these are the same aspects that might make up an offer or request. Offers and requests should be simple and actionable. Simple means that each offer only contains one change from the current stroke such as a change in location or speed, but not both at once. To make an actionable offer or request is to stay out of qualitative and general language. For instance, instead of offering or requesting a "better" or "more resonant" or "different" stroke, make sure the communication is specific and actionable by the stroker.

You'll also want to avoid questions like, "Does this feel good?" or, "Am I doing this right?" or, "What would you like?" These kinds of questions make the strokee think too much. They also might not want to hurt the stroker's feelings, and so withhold the truth. Following these guidelines should help.

CORRECT FORM FOR OFFERS AND REQUESTS:

"Would you like/Can I have a firmer stroke?"
"Would you like/Can I have a slower stroke?"
"Would you like/Can I have a shorter stroke?"
"Would you like/Can I have an upstroke?"
"Would you like me to/Would you move a little to the right?"

When receiving an offer, the strokee can say, "Yes," or, "No." After hearing the yes or no, the stroker says, "Thank you," to acknowledge the communication.

When receiving a request, the stroker can likewise say, "Thank you." The strokee can always decline an offer, but strokers should comply with requests provided the request is within the bounds of the practice.

THE TWO-MINUTE MARK AND FINAL DOWNSTROKES

When there are only two minutes left on the timer, the stroker will announce, "Two minutes." Even if your timer has a chime to note there are two minutes remaining, this is always verbalized. At this point in the OM, both partners prepare for the stroking portion of the OM to come to a close in a few ways. No matter what, the last two minutes should end with both partners feeling more grounded. This is accomplished by using exclusively downstrokes. The two minutes gives a little time to finish a peak gracefully if you're in the middle of one. First, the stroker should use their intuition to feel for how the final two minutes should go.

Commonly, the stroker will taper off the peak they're on, shift to a downstroke, and continue until the strokes become progressively slower, more firm, short-to-medium-length downstrokes using the pad of the finger from the twelve o'clock spot to the six o'clock spot, like a crescendo. So for example, if the stroke had been a fast, light, short upstroke on the ten o'clock spot just before the two-minute mark, the stroker will spend maybe the first thirty seconds or so of the two minutes gradually shifting the stroke to the slower, firmer, short-to-medium-length downstroke. Once you've entered this final, downward descent, one downstroke should take approximately as much time as one full exhalation while breathing normally.

THE END OF THE STROKING PORTION

Continue with the final downstrokes until the final bell sounds on your timer. At this point, stroking stops completely. Once you've stopped stroking, you've successfully completed Step 11.

Step 12. Final Grounding

At this point, the fifteen minutes of stroking have concluded. For final grounding, the stroker places their left hand over their partner's genitals, fingers together, facing downward. They place their right hand over their left, fingers together and pointing upward, and apply firm pressure distributed equally down on the strokee's pubic bone and up toward the strokee's head. The pressure relieves the genital area of engorgement, and, like the other grounding pressure and strokes we've applied throughout the experience, helps smooth out the more energizing quality of the stroking portion of the OM. The final grounding pressure is typically held for between five and ten seconds.

Step 13. The Towel Stroke

The towel stroke employs the washcloth placed under the strokee's genitals. Once the final grounding is complete, the strokee can lift up her hips, at which point the stroker retrieves the towel from under her and folds it in half.

The stroker positions the top of the folded towel lengthwise over their partner's genitals, holding the top of the towel with their left hand. The stroker's right hand is placed on the reverse side of the towel from where it makes genital contact. The stroker's right hand should be more or less over the whole of the front of the introitus and labia.

Gently and with consistency, pull the washcloth upward with the left hand while maintaining pressure with the right hand, as the washcloth collects the lubricant. Be careful not to drag too firmly over the top of the genitals as the towel can feel abrasive to the clitoris. You'll also want to avoid starting too low as fecal matter can contaminate the towel. Once the length of the towel has been completely drawn upward over the strokee's genitals, the stroker opens the towel up and then reverses the fold of the towel, so the lube is now on the inside. Then, the stroker lays the towel over the strokee's genitals and leaves it there.

Step 14. Remove the Gloves

At this point, the stroker removes their gloves: take off one glove by pulling from the wrist inside out over the fingers and bunch it up into the palm of the still-gloved hand, then take off the second glove in the same way with the first glove wrapped inside of it. Discard.

The stroker now offers a hand or arm to assist the strokee up to join them in a seated position.

Step 15. Sharing Frames

Sharing frames is the second-to-last step of the OM. A frame is a brief, value-neutral description of one moment during an experience.

Linguists contend that language shapes our experiences. Without a well-developed set of language skills to help us describe the fleeting sensory experiences of the body, we are less likely to grasp that they have occurred in the first place. The main reason we share frames is to develop a bridge between the feeling, sensory, and linguistic parts of the brain. We have found that finding language, no matter how limited it may be, to describe what we feel and having a way to close out the experience gives each partner more insight into what they felt, and what the other person felt. In a sense, frames help us to digest the rich experiences we just had. Practitioners report that over time they begin to develop a sense of fluency with sensation-based language, and that their ability to discern finer, more subtle elements of their experience greatly increases.

Because we're focused on our connection to the body, in OM, we use the same kind of value-neutral language we learned about in previous steps. For frames, you can use adjectives that are tangible—so for example, descriptions of:

- Temperature
- Speed
- Vibration
- Movement
- Length
- Weight or pressure
- Solidity
- Density
- Texture
- Location

Here are a few examples:

- I had a moment when I felt a hot, fast, light buzzing sensation in my finger.
- I had a moment when I felt a warm, tingly, slow, misty sensation in my stomach.
- I had a moment when I felt a cool, sharp, pointy sensation in my clitoris.

Notice here we spoke about what we did feel, not what we didn't. Keep frames in the positive. Something you didn't feel or expected to feel isn't a sensation, it's a judgment.

During this step, both partners each share one frame. After your partner shares their frame, you can simply say, "Thank you."

So much can happen in an OM. Remember, while you might experience a range of emotions and other observations during the OM, frames are based solely in sensation. Once you're done with the OM and have put away the nest, if you and your partner still want to talk about other aspects of the experience, you're welcome to do so. Once both partners have shared a frame, Step 15 is complete.

Step 16. Clean Up the Nest

After sharing frames, the strokee puts her clothing back on and the nest is broken down. Both partners put away the nest and clean up the supplies. Make sure to store your nest neatly somewhere so it's ready for the next time you OM. Once the nest is put away, Step 16 and your OM are both complete.

Journaling

Have you ever stood in the rain trying to catch falling drops in your mouth? It's difficult to catch even a few, let alone enough for a full drink of water. During an OM, we find ourselves in a similar situation—able to feel a perpetually wider degree of raw sensation that often feels fleeting. OM journaling is the method we use to return to those fleeting moments and become intimate with them.

OM helps us to attune to our bodies. We learn to sense a degree of richness and subtlety we might normally overlook. While we learn to grow our attention and our capacity to notice it all, often there is so much happening it's impossible to track and attend to every single feeling and detail in real time. We share frames at the end of the OM to begin the process of digesting those complex, sensory experiences. The practice of frames is rooted in simplicity—a frame is one moment, like a drop of time, that we communicate in value-neutral language. Because there is so much more that happens—often, several moments and various sensory experiences occur during the OM—than what we can fit into a single frame, this is where journaling comes in.

The process of OM journaling invites us to enter our memories and let them tell us what we were unable to hear when we were bound by time. We take a snapshot of a moment and blow it up to portrait size. We zoom in. Maybe when we try to remember the OM, it feels like a jumble, or maybe we have vivid memories to express. Either way, the practice of OM journaling gives us the opportunity to take a little more time to slow down and revisit each moment, each subtlety, each bit of sensory information, and the impression it left on us.

Like frames, we're pairing the felt-sense impressions of the OM with our mind and vocabulary. You can think of it like the body teaching us its sensory language; each OM offers a new opportunity to discover how the body and the mind want to interact today. We suggest you let it be an exploration: how do you describe that moment when a warm, tingly sensation moves from your pelvis to your chest? Or when a light, feathery heat pulses in your chest? What did you learn about the way you respond to more pressure, or what happened when the stroke quickened?

In an OM journal, we are free to talk about any aspect of the OM we choose and to go into as much detail as we like on our own terms. It could take the form of a play-by-play, or a narrative, or even a conversation. You can choose.

The suggestion is to start small. Pick just one feeling and see how much you can mine it for detail.

ON LANGUAGE AND TERMS

Many people speak multiple extrinsic languages but few have translated the language of gender. Male language is linear, direct, often instructive. Low-level abstractions are preferred. Female language is multidimensional, nonlinear, indirect, relational, and often inquisitive. Studies showed that 99% of both genders speak and understand male language, but only 30% speak or even understand feminine language (of this 99%, 90% are women and a higher concentration of these are African Americans). Feminine reality is encoded in female language yet so few speak it.

The whole field of semantics is what I would consider retraining the world in feminine language style. This is vital because we are building a map of consciousness for uncharted territory, and we can only point to a thousand tiny spotlights. It's a new way of seeing, similar to writing about psychedelics, where there is no existing language to describe certain universal experiences. And let me tell you, it is as complexity mathematician Jim Herriot says, "right side up," meaning our conception of reality is presently upside down.

We will bring a common language to the feminine and the universal experience of Eros. With these Sutras, language forms around the rich, unmapped territory of the feminine experience, giving words to what once could only be felt.

KEY DEFINITIONS

Compensatory

Behaviors or actions we engage in as a way to make up for or compensate for a perceived lack or deficiency. Compensatory behaviors can arise when we are not fully connected to the true nature of our desires. These compensations can manifest in different ways and serve as substitutes or distractions from addressing our deeper needs and desires.

Daimon

An inner voice or guiding force that can help individuals discover their true purpose or calling in life. The realm of the daimonic is linked to life force and creativity and often speaks through intuition and dreams. It is a carrier of your soul's true blueprint and destiny. It will defy the self that is an assemblage of normative cultural behaviors, and bring you the energy needed to break through old conditioning.

Digestion

The alchemical process of converting experiences, feelings, and sensations we have had and that we are storing inside of ourselves into fuel, energy, and wisdom. In order to digest this material, we must descend into our body and remain with experiences, listening and then acting so that we empty out the undigested material we have been holding on to.

Emptiness

A Buddhist term that refers to both a realm of clear light and a way of direct perception. Conceptual presumptions build up through the process of naming and identifying with forms as we are conditioned to see them. When we cut through the perceptual mélange and see things as they are, we notice nothing is added, and nothing is removed from the raw data we encounter.

Eros

An essential energy force that arises from our desire for connection with ourselves, others, and the world around us. It encompasses all of life, evokes beauty, and contributes to an understanding of essential truth. It seeks to unify masculine and feminine energies and manifests as creativity and genius.

Erotic body

The Erotic body refers to the physical body as the vessel for experiencing and expressing Erotic energy. The Erotic body, when functioning properly, works to convert Erotic impulse and desire into life force.

Erotic impulse

The Erotic impulse refers to the raw, unimpeded life force within us that drives our creative expression, spiritual experiences, and desires. It is a potent force and an incorruptible, value-neutral guide that connects us to the world and brings us into an embodied state of being.

Erotic mind

Our intuitive body wisdom that leads us through the lens of desire, longing, and the depth of embodied love. The Erotic mind does not reject anything, but includes all and reveres all of life as sacred.

Erotic self

The Erotic self refers to the unique and essential truth of who we are at our core, beyond societal conditioning and external expectations. The erotic self is intimately connected to our erotic energy and impulse, representing the totality of our being and our unique calling in the world.

Eudaimonia

A Greek word combining the prefix *eu* (meaning good or well) and *daimon* (meaning spirit) describes the state of human flourishing that arises when we act in accord with our nature and live in our "funktionslust" or the "spot" of our soul. It is a virtuous cycle where we receive more power, and in receiving more power we are able to connect more deeply into our purpose.

Homeostatic self

The aspect of ourselves that has been conditioned to react and respond to reality through habitual patterns that are more focused on coping with life rather than penetrating and living the Mystery.

Hydration

Replenishing the body, mind, and spirit. Hydration refers to when we are fully nourished.

Incarnate

To incorporate soul into physical reality.

Interior world

The realm of consciousness that is rooted in the subjective, interior experience of the self. Accessing the interior world is the way we understand ourselves in relationship to the exterior world, and then gain an understanding that they are not ultimately separate. By reflecting on our interior world, we have access to the felt sense of our spiritual development, psychic adulthood, and can take responsibility for our reality.

Introitus

The entrance or opening of the vagina.

Meek

The ancient Greek word for meek, *praus* (πραεῖς), was used to refer to a horse trained for battle. Wild stallions were captured for riding, pulling, and general labor. For these horses, it was essential that their wild nature be broken. Of those horses, there was a set that, despite the best training, always retained a part of that wild nature. These horses were trained, disciplined, and obedient, but never broken. They were unconditional. The stallion that is the "meeked" one, retained his wild nature, is the most obedient to the unalterable truth. Meeked is reserved for the strongest among us. For when the strongest are obedient to unalterable truth, they can endure the weight of compassion and openheartedness.

The Mystery

An ineffable aspect of life that humans perceive but cannot fully comprehend or articulate. The Mystery has been studied and described throughout history by philosophers, theologians, poets, and scientists, but remains elusive and beyond complete understanding. It is often associated with concepts such as God, love, design, sentience, and grace, but all of these names are only temporary and contextual representations of it. It is both eternal and fleeting, beyond human grasp yet a constant presence in the world.

Mystical state

A state of consciousness that is marked by a sense of connection or intimacy with all things stemming from the original Erotic impulse. The mystical state is a state of being that is beyond the rational mind and is often associated with experiences of transcendence, unity, and oneness with the universe.

Nobility

Nobility refers to the inherent quality of a person who is not influenced or defined by temporary thoughts, feelings, or sensory experiences. It is the expression of one's perfection that is waiting to be recognized and embraced as their true identity. Nobility is not something that can be achieved or acquired; rather, it is a fundamental aspect of our being that we must acknowledge and embody.

Optionality

Optionality is a state of being that allows for openness, flexibility, and the ability to respond to life's experiences with a sense of choice and freedom. It is about having a wide range of possibilities available and being able to navigate them with a sense of curiosity and exploration.

Orgasmic Meditation

Orgasmic Meditation (OM) is a structured attention-training practice conducted between two people who are following a predefined set of detailed instructions. The practice involves one person, the stroker, gently stroking the clitoris of the other person, the strokee, for fifteen minutes while both place their attention on the point of contact and notice what they feel.

Overstroke

When we continue to stroke a particular spot, even after the initial charge or freshness has diminished, we are overstroking. Overstroking can happen in OM, in conversation, and in any other aspect of life.

Phase transition

The smooth and seamless experience of transitioning from one state of consciousness to another, rather than a sudden or violent change. This transition is seen as a natural and integral part of the flow of Eros, and is characterized by a sense of liberation and release.

Power

The manifesting aspect of reality that can be accessed through surrender to Eros. Power is an animation that originates outside of our homeostatic self and enacts itself through us, carrying with it the ability to direct or organize psychic energy. Unlike force, power fuels, activates, and catalyzes ourselves, others, and the world.

Profane

The profane can be seen as the ordinary, everyday aspects of life and may be overlooked or dismissed as lacking in significance. However, within the profane exists the potential for the sacred to be found. The profane and the sacred are not opposing forces; they are interconnected aspects of existence. The profane is not separate from the sacred, but is rather a different expression or manifestation of it.

Pumping

Pumping is a compensatory behavior where individuals seek increasing intensity or impact in order to feel a sense of satisfaction or fulfillment. It is a way of trying to generate a desired outcome through forceful or excessive effort. This can manifest in various aspects of life, including sexual experiences, emotional interactions, or even in the pursuit of personal goals.

Residue

Residue refers to the mental and emotional remnants or traces of thoughts, memories, or projections that distract from being fully present in the moment and engaged in the practice. Residue occurs when we leap into an imagined future or replay the past, taking away from the pure experience we are in.

Safeport

A safeport is when we tell someone what we are going to do before we do it. We safeport in OM before making physical contact with our partner just as we safeport in communications with people at various times. Safeporting isn't asking for permission; it is telling someone what we are going to do and when.

Sensation

Sensation is the way we experience and interpret the world around us, as well as our internal states. It is the raw, embodied experience of feeling and perceiving. Not limited to just physical touch or sensory perception, it also includes emotional and energetic sensations. It is the language through which intimacy and connection are communicated.

The spot

A specific point of activation in the body that is associated with the experience of Eros or Erotic energy. It is described as a physical and energetic location that, when touched or stroked in a specific way, can lead to a profound sense of connection and spiritual awakening. Finding and cultivating a relationship with the spot is essential for experiencing the full potential of Eros and for living a life of deep fulfillment and purpose. The spot is described as being uncompromising and absolute, with no room for "almost" or "close." It is a binary experience that is either on or off, and anything less than being fully on the spot is considered a compensation for not being in the fullness of Eros.

Stroke

An action or communication made toward another person. In OM, a stroke refers to the motion of the finger on the clitoris. Outside of OM, a stroke is a communication delivered with intention, which can be either verbal or an action, directed at an individual, group of people, or an enterprise.

Strokee

The strokee is the person whose clitoris is being stroked during the practice of OM. In the context of a conversation, strokee refers to the person who is receiving the attention or focus of the discussion. They are the ones being "stroked" through the conversation, similar to how they would be in an OM session. The strokee's role is not passive but rather an active engagement with their own body and the sensations that arise.

Stroker

The stroker is the person stroking the strokee's clitoris during the practice of OM. In the context of a conversation, the stroker refers to the individual who is actively guiding or directing the conversation. The stroker strokes using their attention. In OM, the stroker does this with their finger; in conversation, through words and responses.

Totality

All aspects of oneself, including the hidden, unexplored, or suppressed parts. Totality includes mind, body, and spirit—physical, psychological, and spiritual components. The whole is always greater than the sum of the parts.

Trauma

A form of tumescence (value-neutral congestion) that, instead of being seen as potential power, is cast as a pathology producing a cycle of shame. Trauma is often related to a particular experience in which the flow of desire was restricted, though with time the congestion may accumulate and aggregate to be reexperienced in a variety of circumstances.

Undigested material

Feelings and sensations that have not been fully processed by the mind and are left unattended and densely packed in the body. This can create a sense of discomfort or unease that can make it difficult to feel in control. However, when you take the time to process these experiences, they can become fuel, energy, and wisdom.

THE EROS SUTRAS VOLUMES

VOLUME 1
PRINCIPLES

◆

VOLUME 2
TUMESCENCE

◆

VOLUME 3
ORGASMIC MEDITATION

◆

VOLUME 4
RELATIONSHIP

◆

VOLUME 5
LIBERATION & JUSTICE

Made in United States
North Haven, CT
07 February 2025

65502681R00153